How to Understand

The

New Testament

Discovering the Uncompromised Gospel

By Lewis J. Tauzeni

How to Understand The New Testament: Discovering the uncompromised Gospel

Copyright © 2021 by Lewis J Tauzeni

ISBN: 978-0-620-92596-9

Reloaded Publishers
Printed in Pretoria, South Africa
Email: reloadoscar@gmail.com
Call: +2773 529 1603

For more of my work and contacts:
Email: howtounderstandthenewcovenant@gmail.com
Books:
TiTHiNG: The Greatest Con of all Time-VII Shocking Secrets About The Old Testament Tithe

TABLE OF CONTENTS

Preface

This is my story: how the journey began...
I have been a Christian for almost 20 years now and have spent most of those years as a New Converts teacher. Over the years, I got to a point where I could not teach Tithing with a clear conscience ***(Be that as it may, this book isn't about tithing)***. This all started while I was doing a personal Bible study on the book of Hebrews. Then I came upon Hebrews 7:5 *"The Law of Moses required Levi to collect a tithe from his brethren."* I could not reconcile what this verse was saying with what I had been taught and came to accept as truth. ***I had been taught and was teaching others that the tithe was not a part of the Law of Moses but was just merely incorporated into the Law***. In short, tithing was not a requirement of the Law. But all to my surprise, here was this verse saying that Tithing was *indeed* a requirement of the Law of Moses!

I had read this particular text and the whole book on countless occasions, but on that fateful day, this verse really struck me and got stuck in my head. This was because I had always known that the book was written to a Jewish Christian audience and that the author of the book was well adept at elucidating Old Testament scriptures. This implied that both the author and his intended audience were well aware of this biblical fact, that Tithing is a requirement of the Law of Moses. That is why the writer even mentions this in passing!

It was therefore next to impossible that the author of the book of Hebrews could have been mistaken on this one. The only clear and logical explanation was the ugly truth that, contrary to what I had been taught and led to believe, tithing was indeed a requirement of the Law! This verse has been slowly eating me away for the past decade or so.

This ultimately forced me to seek the Lord in prayer and also carry out my own research into the Doctrine of Tithing. One of the fundamental principles of this doctrine is the understanding that tithing was never a requirement of the Law but that it was *merely included* or rather **incorporated** into the Law of Moses. Since *Tithing started in Genesis with Father Abraham, it is therefore not Law.* But here was a biblical text that clearly stated otherwise. I started going over all the proof texts on tithing and I was confronted with the ugly reality that the whole doctrine on Tithing is not congruent with the Gospel that was handed down to us by the Apostles.

I then discovered that the Tithe or tithing is just a tiny needle in the haystack! In fact, most of what appears to be mainstream theology of today's Christian Church does not comply with the Gospel. The mere fact that the doctrine of Tithing has been gladly accepted by the Christian community across the whole divide, just shows how as a Church we have all lost our way. This is what has ultimately inspired me to write this book.

Introduction

This book explores the theological basis of all New Testament doctrine. This is more of a *How-To-Guide* on how to separate or distinguish true from false gospel or false teachings under the New Testament Church. The bulk of the Christian doctrines we use in Church today are compromised as a result of failing to accurately handle the truth of God in the Old Testament scriptures. Christianity is now full of people who know denominational doctrines and possess a somewhat twisted understanding of the scriptures.

It seems believers across the globe choose to understand scriptures in line with how their Church denomination interprets them! This is what we call in general terms, indoctrination. People know more and hold onto what their 'church' teaches and not what the bible actually says. Most of what people perceive to be what the scriptures say, is nothing but the doctrines of men. I have since learnt through the guidance of the Holy Spirit that there is a very thin line between *truth and belief*. One should never believe a thing simply because *they want* it to be true but rather, one must believe in something because it's true.

As Christians our belief must be established on truth and not the other way around! Something must be true for you to believe in it. Belief doesn't always determine the truthfulness of something. One may sincerely believe in either a truth or a lie, so just because you believe it doesn't imply that it's true! The point that I am trying to put across is that it is very possible to believe in a lie. Therefore, it's imperative that all doctrines be guided by truth and never belief. We should therefore seek to augment truth in our doctrines and not just belief (Acts17:11).

Many are now being driven by belief and not truth. For that reason, if one becomes aware that their doctrine is incorrect, they will still cling to it, because they believe in it! It's very dangerous to just base on belief when it comes to matters on doctrine verification. Even though Jews had certain beliefs about worshipping God, the Berean Jews chose to search the scriptures so as to ascertain whether or not what Paul said was true. Doctrine is verified with scripture and not just belief!

As a result, there seems to be so much confusion on things that a Christian ought to do to be saved and to please the Lord under the New Covenant. Most of the confusion or false doctrines that have perverted the true Gospel of our Lord Jesus Christ, has largely been the result of developing doctrines on Gentile Christianity basing on Old Testament scriptures. As shall be revealed later, most of the false teachers who were denounced by the Apostles, derived their teachings from their understanding of the Law.

I am strongly under the impression that, before reading the Bible one should be given all the information on how to best apply it in their walk of faith. On the contrary, we are just encouraged to read the whole Bible from cover to cover and from there one is expected to then decipher how to live the life of a good Christian! This is not as easy as it sounds because the Christian Bible contains manuals for two religions, Judaism and Christianity. The Old Testament provides a complete guide on Judaism and the New Testament a complete guide on Christianity.

This then indicates that not everything recorded in the Bible is for Christians in general and uncircumcised Christians in particular! Just because something is in the Bible, doesn't infer that it can be practiced or taught to Christians (burnt offerings). While Christianity has its roots in Judaism, Gentile Christian doctrine formulation is exclusively confined to the New Testament portion of the Bible. In other words, the Apostolic letters are more authoritative in matters of all Gentile Christian doctrine than the Old Testament scriptures. While we can derive some lessons from how Jews interacted with God in the Old Testament scriptures, our doctrines must be derived and be guided by the instructions from the Apostles to the New Testament Church of Christ!

There are just too many doctrines and denominations, the whole entire Christendom is in an alarming chaotic state. The situation is now so dire and has reached a point where if someone tries to point out all these anomalies and inconsistencies in the bulk of the many perceived Christian doctrines, he or she becomes the agent of the Devil! This is what has motivated me to write this book, so that every child of God out there can read the word of God by themselves.

That they may also learn to understand how to apply the truth contained therein, appropriately in their walk of faith.

We must no longer be guided or tossed to and fro by the traditions of men. For one to have an idea of what this book is all about, let me ask you this very simple question. If we are to give you just the teachings of the Apostles to the Gentiles, will you still come to the same conclusions about your Church doctrine? It must be noted that God spoke long ago, against false teachings through his Apostles and how these false teachings may pervert the gospel of Christ. God does not have to speak again in some other way on false teachings and false gospels! This simply implies that we need to be in a position to identify false teachings and how these false teachings pervert the gospel of Christ.

In this book, I proffer some guidelines on how we may understand the theological basis of all New Testament Church doctrine. I shall reveal how some have gone astray in their pursuit to please God because of failure to fully comprehend the gospel message as handed down by the Apostles; the significance of the death of our Lord Jesus at Calvary and how to accurately integrate Old Testament Scriptures in our doctrines and walk of faith.

I wrote this book by the grace that God has given me, it's not by my own might or wisdom, but simply GRACE. Glory be to God, the Father of our Lord Jesus Christ...

Chapter 1

How do we draw the Line between the Old and the New Testament?

*"In the case of a will, it is necessary to prove the death of the one who made it, because a will is only in force, only when somebody has died; **it never takes effect while the one who made it is still living**. That is why even the first Covenant was not put into effect without blood."*
Hebrews 9:16-18

Over the centuries, the lines between the two covenants have become too obscured to such an extent that nobody is sure of anything anymore. Do the two Covenants overlap? Do they co-exist? Does one abolish the other? Most of what we call Christian doctrine has been a result of how one understands these questions. Consequently, Christianity now has a myriad of doctrines and some common ground in-between. But no doubt, the main reason why Christianity is polarized is because of our understanding or misunderstanding of both Covenants and our failure to accurately demarcate the line between the two.

The main divisive issue has always been on the application of the Old Testament truth in our walk of faith as uncircumcised Gentile Christians in particular. To what extent does the Old Covenant truth affect our relationship with God? Even so, before we go there, one must possess a general appreciation of the Old Testament. One very distinctive aspect of the Old Testament is the influence that was wielded by the Prophet

Moses (Deuteronomy 18:18). A close scrutiny of the Old Testament will reveal that while we have so many prophets, there is only one authoritative figure in the entire Testament, and that figure is Moses. It is what Moses said or prescribed that stood. Moses' role in mediating and establishing the Old Covenant was so climactic that the whole Covenant is widely known as the Mosaic Law or the Law of Moses!

However, some might argue that the Commandments that were given in the Old Covenant were God's Law and did not come from Moses the person. The irony in that statement is that whoever says or teaches that forgets that even our Lord Jesus Christ at times referred to the Law as **"the Law of Moses"** on many occasions for example *Luke 24:44, 'He said to them, "This is what I told you while I was still with you: Everything must be fulfilled that is written about me in the **Law of Moses**, the Prophets and the Psalms." Mark 1:44 "...But go, show yourself to the priest and offer the sacrifices that **Moses commanded** for your cleansing..."*

The Apostles and Pharisees referred to the Law as the *'Law of Moses.' Acts 15:5 "Then some of the believers who belonged to the party of the Pharisees stood up and said, 'The Gentiles must be circumcised and required to obey the **Law of Moses'."** This phrase in essence punctuates both the Old and New Testament writings. The Apostle Paul who was also a Pharisee before his conversion regularly used this phrase as well *1Corinthians 9:9 **"For it is written in the Law of Moses**: "Do not muzzle an ox while it is treading out the grain." Also, the writer of Hebrews wrote, "Anyone who rejected the **law**

11

of Moses died without mercy on the testimony of two or three witnesses." Hebrews 10:28

Moses is the Authoritative figure of the Old Covenant

Why did the Jews refer to the Old Covenant Law as the *'Law of Moses?'* They did that because Moses is the Authority of the Old Covenant. The reason is very clear, simple, and straightforward. He is the one who received the **REVELATION**, mediated, and established the Old Covenant. Everything that Moses commanded, prescribed, or decreed, he received by direct revelation from God. He is the one who gave the instruction on how Israel could serve and worship YAHWEH! It is what Moses commanded that regulated Israel's lifestyle from religion, politics, social and economics. All these were codified in the 5 books of the Law that are now popularly known as the Pentateuch or simply the **Torah**: *Genesis, Exodus, Leviticus, Numbers and Deuteronomy*!

To clearly illustrate that Moses is indeed the Authority of the Old Testament, let me give reference to an exchange that Jesus had with the teachers of the Law concerning divorce.

> *"Some Pharisees came to him to test him. They asked, "Is it lawful for a man to divorce his wife for any and every reason?" …. vs3*
> *"Why then," they asked, "did Moses command that a man give his wife a certificate of divorce and send her away?" Jesus replied, "Moses permitted you to divorce your wives because your hearts were hard. But it was not this way from the beginning."*
> *Matthew 19:7-8*

This was a very interesting exchange indeed. As already alluded to, Moses was the Authoritative figure of the Old

12

Covenant as such the Pharisees tried to entrap Jesus using what Moses had commanded. They asked him a question so that they could twist whatever he would say and use it against him. The one thing that captivated me was that both parties acknowledged the fact that *it was Moses who gave the command*! Simply because he possessed the **divine revelatory *Authority*** to do so. Even Jesus also acknowledged the same fact and pointed out that Moses had indeed through *his own discretion, **permitted*** them to divorce their wives! There is no mention of God in this exchange! As one endued with the *Revelatory Authority* of the Old Covenant, everything Moses commanded and decreed became God's Law because he was the one who possessed the revelation.

The authoritative figure of the Old Testament is very much known, that is why it is not difficult to settle any differences or disputes when it comes to the Old Testament. An enquiry is made as to what the Law of Moses says with regards to the given dispute and whatever the Law says settles the matter. No one disputes Moses's revelation of the Old Covenant, which revelation he put into writing, and served as the authoritative source for all Old Testament worship. Israelite worship was regulated by the Law of Moses. Even Old Testament prophecy was Covenant specific or Covenant oriented. Prophets enforced and were custodians of the Law!

This is the primary reason why we have so much discord in the body of Christ today. There is no uniformity of doctrine simply because the Body of Christ has not yet identified the authoritative figure of the New Testament especially among the Gentile Christians!

Where does the New Testament begin?

This seems to be a very simple and straight forward question which requires a very simple answer. If one opens their Bible, all that they need to do is turn to the section of the Bible that's written the New Testament and that's it. If one opens their Bible on Mathew 1:1 and Walla... they would already be in the New Testament! Much of the confusion we have in the Universal Church today, is largely attributed to our mishandling of the message that is conveyed in the Gospels. Hence, for us to clearly grasp the message in the gospels, we must first understand their *historical timeline*.

While the Gospels are classified as **Christian writings** because they were written specifically for a Christian audience, they contain a record of events that took place before the New Testament took effect! All the events that are recorded in the four gospels transpired under an *Old Testament setting*. This shows that **the New Testament did not begin at the birth of Jesus**. Or in other words the Birth of Jesus did not signal the end of the Old Testament or even the beginning of the New! The Gospels are more biographical in nature. The Apostle Paul pointed out that:

> *"Jesus was born under the Law in order to redeem those that were under the Law..." Galatians 4:4-5.*

It is fundamental to know and understand that the New Testament doesn't start at Matthew 1:1. The New Testament only started or took effect *after the death of Jesus* and not any time before! Jesus was born under the Law, was circumcised on the 8th day, thus he observed the Law of Moses in order to fulfill it. Hence, *Jesus fulfilled the Law by what he said or did and then abolished it by what he did on the cross*! Once we understand this, we can no longer have any misunderstandings about what Jesus said or did. Jesus, being a Jew was born under the Law and had to fulfill the Law in word and in deed.

*"For this reason, **Christ is the mediator of a New Covenant...now that he had died as ransom** to set them free from the sins committed under the first Covenant. In the case of a will, it is necessary to prove the death of the one who made it, because a will is only in force, only when somebody has died; **it never takes effect while the one who made it is still living**. That is why even the first Covenant was not put into effect without blood"*
Hebrews 9:15-18
*"**If he were on earth, he would not be a priest,** for there are already men who offer the gifts prescribed by the law." Hebrews 8:4*

The above given scriptures ratify the fact that Jesus Christ is the mediator of the New Covenant. He only assumed this role of High priest and mediator after his death. For Jesus could not perform this duty of mediation and assuming his priesthood while on earth because there were men who were already performing this priestly duty in line with the requirement of the Law of Moses. The New Covenant did not take or could not take effect while the Testator was still alive. It was through death and his blood, which he offered as the once and for all time sacrifice in the Heavenly sanctuary that put the New Covenant into effect.

The Old Covenant was abolished, and the New Covenant took effect by what Jesus did when he died and not at His birth or any time prior. Whatever Jesus said or did, he did so while fulfilling the Law. He couldn't qualify to be the perfect lamb of God if he had not fulfilled the Law in word and in deed. In order to fulfill the Law, he had to teach those that lived under the Law how to obey it in a manner that God had intended. He couldn't have acted otherwise. We must therefore note that Jesus did not abolish the Old Covenant by what he said, Jesus only abolished the Law of Moses when he died on the cross.

Possessing this information would then help us to correctly apply the truth about what Jesus said or did in our walk of faith. I have also outlined how we may correctly demarcate the boundary between the two Covenants. *The death of Jesus Christ is the dividing line between the two covenants.* Failure to appreciate the difference between the two and the dividing line between them can be catastrophic especially when it concerns doctrine formulation. Can one come up with a doctrine that Jesus came to save the lost sheep of Israel only, because of these verses in Matthew?

'These twelve Jesus sent out with the following instructions: **"Do not go among the Gentiles or enter any town of the Samaritans**. Go rather to the lost sheep of Israel."* Matthew 10:5-6

'He answered, "I was sent only to the lost sheep of Israel." Matthew 15:24

Chapter 2

Jewish Christians and the Law of Moses

'Then they said to Paul: "You see, brother, how many thousands of Jews have believed, and all of them are zealous for the law. They have been informed that you teach all the Jews who live among the Gentiles to turn away from Moses, telling them not to circumcise their children or live according to our customs."
Acts 21:17-21

First, we need to determine whether or not there was an overlap between the two Covenants. This is because there are some who have observed how the Jewish Christians were predisposed to the Law of Moses and then concluded that the two Covenants overlap or at most core-exist. However, a careful study through the book of Acts will reveal that we have two main groups of Christians under the early New Testament Church, Jewish (Circumcised) and Gentile (Uncircumcised) Christians. Understanding the difference between these two main groups will settle this issue once and for all.

There were three types of Jewish Christians or the *"circumcised brothers"*; namely, the **Hebraic Jews**, who were Hebrew speaking and had lived in Israel all their lives; the **Hellenic Jews**, who were Greek speaking Jews from the diaspora and those who had settled back in Israel; then the **Gentiles** who had converted to Judaism or simply the Jewish proselytes. Accordingly, understanding the difference between these two main groups of Christians; the *Circumcised brothers* and the uncircumcised will also help us discover the uncompromised Gospel.

Honestly, I do not know how many times I have read the first few chapters of Acts and this plain truth has always eluded me. The first Church at Jerusalem was all pro-Jewish or was made up of the three groups mentioned above: Hebraic Jews, Hellenic Jews, and Jewish proselytes. This is particularly true because the events at Pentecost took place during the annual Jewish feast of Pentecost. As was their custom Jews from all over Israel and those from the diaspora as well as Gentile converts to Judaism thronged Jerusalem for such a big annual religious festival.

*"Now there were staying in Jerusalem **God-fearing Jews from every nation under heaven**. When they heard this sound, a crowd came together in bewilderment, because each one heard their own language being spoken. Utterly amazed, they asked: "Aren't all these who are speaking Galileans? Then how is it that each of us hears them in our native language? Parthians, Medes and Elamites; residents of Mesopotamia, Judea and Cappadocia, Pontus and Asia, Phrygia and Pamphylia, Egypt and the parts of Libya near Cyrene; visitors from Rome **(both Jews and converts to Judaism)**; Cretans and Arabs—we hear them declaring the wonders of God in our own tongues!"... "Then Peter stood up with the Eleven, raised his voice and addressed the crowd: **"Fellow Jews** and all of you who live in Jerusalem, let me explain this to you; listen carefully to what I say."*
Acts 2v5-11;14

It is quite embarrassing to admit that for years I had been under the impression that uncircumcised *Gentiles* were also present at Pentecost and I'm pretty sure that I wasn't alone in this! One would know just how ridiculous this sounds if they were fully aware of Jewish customs. Nonetheless, the above text clearly shows that the events of Acts Two were of a purely Jewish setting. The Church at Jerusalem was made up of Jewish Christians only. All the events from the first ten or so chapters of Acts are that of Jewish Christians. All the altercations that took place between the Apostles and the Jewish Sanhedrin, how the Apostles were forbidden to preach or teach in the name of Jesus etc. The first Church at Jerusalem was Jewish, and the only Gentiles present were all converts to Judaism. Thus, they were already circumcised and observed the law before Pentecost.

Being aware of this very tiny insignificant detail is the key to unraveling the New Covenant! One will also discover that Jewish Christians or the circumcised brothers continued observing the Law of Moses and Jewish customs! While we may not be certain to what extent they did so, it is on record that Jewish Christians observed the Law of Moses. The first incident that reveals this New Testament Church reality would obviously be that of Peter and Cornelius. This was well after the New Testament had taken full effect, Jesus had died and resurrected, and the Holy Spirit had descended.

Peter received a strange vision, whereby The Lord gave him what appeared to be a very weird instruction, one that was at odds with his Jewish roots:

*"About noon the following day as they were on their journey and approaching the city, Peter went up on the roof to pray. He became hungry and wanted something to eat, and while the meal was being prepared, he fell into a trance. He saw heaven opened and something like a large sheet being let down to earth by its four corners. It contained **all kinds** of four-footed animals, as well as reptiles and birds. Then a voice told him, **"Get up, Peter. Kill and eat." "Surely not, Lord!"** Peter replied. **"I have never eaten anything impure or unclean."** The voice spoke to him a second time, **"Do not call anything impure that God has made clean."***
Acts 10:9-15

Peter was given an instruction from Heaven to kill anything and eat. He then responded by pointing out that he had never eaten *anything "unclean"* all his life. *(Please note that after the Holy Spirit had descended signifying that the New Testament had taken full effect, didn't imply that Peter and the other Jewish Christians started eating pork etc.).* It went on for about three times, Peter being offered and then he would refuse! Of course, the underlying message behind this vision wasn't for Peter or the other Jewish Christians to start eating unclean meat, but rather to change his mind or their attitude towards *"uncircumcised"* Gentiles in general.

This incident clearly reveals the Jewish attitude toward the *"uncircumcised"* Gentiles. This attitude was because of what the Law of Moses instructed. An attitude which would probably have prevented the Jewish Christians from preaching the gospel to the uncircumcised Gentiles. If our Lord had not confronted Peter in a vision, it would have been very difficult for him to accept that an angel of the Lord had appeared to an uncircumcised Gentile and let alone agree to accompany Cornelius's men to his home!

So, when Peter saw Cornelius's men, it was then that he understood what the vision meant, so he went with them without asking any questions. This is what he said to Cornelius upon entering his house.

*"While talking with him, Peter went inside and found a large gathering of people. He said to them: "You are well aware that it is **against our law for a Jew to associate with or visit a Gentile**. But God has shown me that I should not call anyone impure or unclean. So when I was sent for, I came without raising any objection. May I ask why you sent for me?"*
Acts 10:27-29

Peter pointed out that it was against **"our law"** for him to visit and even enter a house of a Gentile(uncircumcised). Here, he was referring to **the Law of Moses**! He said this to let them know that he would be in serious trouble for doing what he had done, with his own people. *First*, he confessed that he had never eaten anything unclean and *secondly*, he admits that he was bound by what the Law of Moses said about interacting with uncircumcised Gentiles! There you have it from the horse's mouth! After Peter had returned from Cornelius' house, he came under serious criticism from fellow Christians who accused him of entering an uncircumcised Gentile's home and even dinning with them.

The believers were totally incensed, despite the fact that they had heard that the uncircumcised Gentiles had received the Holy Spirit! The circumcised Christians took great offence at what Apostle Peter had done. They were more worried about upholding the Law of Moses to such an extent that even news of uncircumcised Gentiles receiving the Holy Spirit seemed totally insignificant!

"The apostles and the believers throughout Judea heard that the Gentiles also had received the word of God. So when Peter went up to Jerusalem, **the circumcised believers criticized him and said,** *"You went into the house of uncircumcised men and ate with them."*
Acts 11:1-3

The mere fact that these believers had to criticize Peter for violating the Law, clearly reveals their attitude towards the Law. Indicating how the whole Church at Jerusalem had initially taken the news of Peter preaching to uncircumcised Gentiles. This also explains why after the persecution that ensued after Stephen's martyrdom; most of the believers who fled from Jerusalem went about witnessing to Jews only!

"Now those who had been scattered by the persecution in connection with Stephen traveled as far as Phoenicia, Cyprus and Antioch, telling the **message only to Jews.**" *Acts 11:19*

Additional evidence from the book of Acts which shows that Jewish Christians continued observing the Law of Moses is found in Acts 21 and this will put the nail on the coffin. What is particularly intriguing about this episode is the exchange that took place between Paul, James, and the Elders of the Church at Jerusalem.

"The next day Paul and the rest of us went to see James, and all the elders were present. Paul greeted them and reported in detail what God had done among the **Gentiles through his ministry.** *When they heard this, they praised God. Then they said to Paul:* **"You see, brother, how many thousands of Jews have believed, and all of them are zealous for the law.** *They have been informed that you teach* **all the Jews** *who live among the Gentiles* **to turn away from Moses, telling them not to circumcise their children or live according to our customs.**" *Acts 21:17-21*

The major take from this text being that James fully acknowledges the fact and puts the whole matter to rest. He points out that the Jewish Christians were **very zealous for the Law**, particularly circumcision and other Jewish customs according to the Law of Moses. Notice that the Church leaders were more worried about how the other Jewish Christians would react once they had learnt of Paul's arrival in Jerusalem. A false report had gone around that Paul was teaching **Jewish Christian**s living among the Gentiles not to circumcise their children or live according to Jewish customs.

In their effort to appease or placate the Jewish Christian Community, James and the elders recommended that Paul should carry out the cleansing ceremony in keeping with the Law of Moses, since he was coming back from Gentile territory. Participating in this rite, would prove to the Jewish Christian community that the report they had heard about Paul was false and that he indeed **observed** the Law of Moses. Hoping to silence Paul's critics in the Church, the Leadership "ordered" Paul to carry out the *cleansing ceremony* as prescribed by the Law of Moses (Numbers 6:9-12).

Now this is an interesting development, this cleansing ceremony was officiated by priests and involved offering burnt sacrifices at the alter in the temple! The Apostles could not officiate over this practice, hence Paul had to go present himself and his delegation to the priests at the Temple. Paul was instructed to join two fellow Christians in their purification rites and was advised to pay for all the sacrifices as a gesture of goodwill on his part!

According to all the above-given scriptural references, it is beyond speculation that Jewish Christians continued observing the Law of Moses. As such, books like the gospel of Matthew for instance, were written for a Jewish Christian audience. There are other books as well such as the book of James, Hebrews, and the greater part of Revelation. While the book of Romans addressed both circumcised and uncircumcised Christians in the Churches in Rome. All these books were penned to a Jewish Christian audience, this now explains a lot concerning the theological background of these books.

This knowledge or understanding is just indispensable in our pursuit towards understanding the uncompromised Gospel of our Lord Jesus Christ to the Gentiles. There are countless teachings and instructions that were given to New Testament Jewish Christians, which teachings aren't compatible with an uncircumcised Gentile audience or Gentile Christians. The relevance or significance of such teachings must be understood within the Jewish Christian context.

As shall be revealed later, the mere fact Jewish Christians continued observing the Law of Moses doesn't imply a covenantal overlap in as far as uncircumcised Christian worship was concerned. Our doctrine as uncircumcised Christians should not be determined or guided by how the Jewish Christians chose to assimilate Judaism in their worship. They continued observing the Law of Moses and Jewish customs for the simple reason that they were Jews!

Chapter 3

Why did Jesus Send Paul to the Gentiles?

"I am talking to you Gentiles. Inasmuch as I am the apostle to the Gentiles, I take pride in my ministry."
Romans 11:13

Why did our Lord Jesus choose Paul to be the Apostle to the Gentiles? That's the question that brews in my ever-inquisitive mind. An Apostle simply means *"One sent"*. Matthew 28v18-20 ends with the risen Christ clearly giving the disciples the charge to go and preach the Gospel to all Nations. Yet in the book of Acts, we have a record of how at first the Apostles or Jewish Christians in general, were reluctant to preach to uncircumcised Gentiles because of the restrictions that were imposed on them by the Law of Moses. Our Lord had to intervene by communicating to Peter via a vision and sending messengers from Cornelius for him to go and preach to uncircumcised Gentiles!

The incident of the Ethiopian Eunuch and Philip is not much to go on. For starters, he was already a Jewish proselyte who was on his way to his homeland from Jerusalem and was reading the book of Isaiah! These were the kind of people the Jewish Christians only witnessed to. Nevertheless, [*probably after hearing about what had happened at Cornelius' house*] some Jews [*emboldened*] went about preaching to Greeks.

Quite a significant number turned to the Lord, hence the birth of the first pro-Gentile Church was at Antioch. The Apostles were alerted of this development and immediately dispatched Barnabas.

My presumption is that the Church at Jerusalem decided to send Barnabas because he was more **suited** for the job. Barnabas was a Hellenic (Greek Speaking) Jew from Cyprus, unlike all the other Apostles, he was more exposed to the Gentile or Pagan lifestyle. The other Apostles had very little exposure to uncircumcised Gentiles. When Barnabas arrived at Antioch, he saw that the report was true, indeed many Gentiles had turned to the Lord. He then went to Tarsus in search of Paul and brought him to Antioch. Then the rest is history.

This was how things were before Paul came into the picture. With everything that unfolded, from where I am standing, it appears as though the Apostles or Jewish Christians in general did not yet understand the Gentile Ministry. They might have known their way when it came to consolidating Judaism with Christianity in as far as the circumcised believer was concerned, but when It came to the uncircumcised Gentiles, it was a totally different story. I have accentuated some of the pitfalls and obstacles that the 11 Apostles faced or had to go through concerning the Gentile Ministry.

It is against this background, that I now fully understand why our Lord Jesus had to send Paul to the Gentiles, not Peter, James, or any of the Apostles whom he walked with.

"On the contrary, they saw that I had been entrusted with the task of preaching the gospel to the Gentiles, just as Peter had been to the Jews. James, Peter, and John, those reputed to be pillars, gave me and Barnabas the right hand of fellowship when they recognized the grace given to me. They agreed that we should go to the Gentiles, and they to the Jews".
Galatians.2:7

Over the years, I have always marveled at the all surpassing wisdom of our Savior. He sent Apostle Peter, who was basically unschooled in the Law of Moses to be the Apostle to the Jews, the people who had the Law. Whereas Paul who was well educated in the Law of Moses and had even attained the office of a Pharisee, a qualified teacher of the Jewish Law, to be the Apostle to the Gentiles, a people who did not have the Law! Shouldn't it have been the other way around? Since Paul was better educated in the Law of Moses, shouldn't he be the Apostle to the Jews and then Peter, who was untrained in the Law, be the Apostle to the Gentiles? That would have made great sense, wouldn't it?

"For the foolishness of God, is great wisdom among men..."
1 Corinthians. 1:25a

"On the contrary, they saw that I had been entrusted with the task of preaching the gospel to the Gentiles, just as Peter had been to the Jews."
Galatians 2:7

I shall try to answer this very pertinent question to the best of my ability. We have already glimpsed the chaos that rocked the church when the uncircumcised Gentile fold was introduced. The whole church was in sixes-and-sevens, nobody really understood what had to be done with the uncircumcised Gentiles. But before we can understand why

Paul was chosen, we must first understand the man he was before being chosen and what he had to go through, before he eventually became Paul, the Apostle to the Gentiles.

If one fails to understand the man Saul, the Jewish Pharisee, and the persecutor of the Church, it would equally be difficult to then grasp the theology of the man Paul, the Apostle to the Gentiles. He was first mentioned at the martyrdom of Stephen. When the people were busy stoning Steven, they threw their cloaks at Saul's feet so that they could adequately pelt Stephen without any hindrance. That is how he is introduced to us. Paul watched with deep satisfaction as Stephen, the blasphemer was stoned to death. Saul was thoroughly assuaged by the death of Stephen that he was invigorated to unleash persecution on the Christians in Jerusalem with so much intensity.

*"But Saul **began to destroy the church.** Going from house to house, he dragged off both men and women and put them in prison."*
Acts 8:3

This unleashed the first wave of persecution that was spearheaded by Saul. This man almost single handedly destroyed the church, he was ruthless in his approach. He went after the Believers door-to-door and dragged them off both men and women to prison. The man, Saul was so devastatingly ruthless that most disciples fled from Jerusalem and scattered across Israel and beyond. Some of them might have fled to Damascus and he got wind of it.

The man was so motivated that he personally went to see the High Priest and asked for letters that would authorize him to arrest all the disciples he might find in all the Synagogues in Damascus and drag them back to Jerusalem. Chapter six records that there were more than five thousand men, and even more were turning to the Lord each day. Saul either arrested most of them or drove them out of Jerusalem!

*"Meanwhile, Saul was still breathing out murderous threats against the Lord's disciples. **He went to the high priest and asked him for letters to the synagogues in Damascus,** so that if he found any there who belonged to the Way, whether men or women, he might take them as prisoners to Jerusalem." Acts 9:1-2*

While on his way to Damascus so that he could deal with the *'blasphemous Nazarenes'*, the Lord Jesus appeared to him!

'He fell to the ground and heard a voice say to him, "Saul, Saul, why do you persecute me?" "Who are you, Lord?" Saul asked. "I am Jesus, whom you are persecuting," he replied.'
Acts 9:4-5

But then again, what was it that was motivating him? Why did Saul persecute the disciples with such viciousness and intensity? Was this a mere sycophantic attempt to ingratiate himself with the Sanhedrin or the High Priest? If we can all appreciate why Saul persecuted believers, it would then be easier to understand his theology. We need not wonder, because he later explained his earlier actions and what exactly it was that motivated him in those days.

*"For you have heard of my **previous** way of life in **Judaism**, how intensely I persecuted the church of God and tried to destroy it. I was advancing in Judaism beyond many of my own age among my people and **was extremely zealous for the traditions of my fathers**."*
Galatians 1:13-14

By his own admission, Paul testified to the Galatians that he intensely persecuting the Church of God and that he was quite intent on destroying it. True to his word, he almost did until he was confronted by our Lord. He had even advanced himself in Judaism beyond his peers and was extremely zealous for the Jewish customs. He also stated that all this happened in his *former* life in Judaism! Notice that Paul used such terms as *Judaism* and *traditions* of my fathers in describing that former life. This is the same thing, but Paul used them interchangeably for emphasis, for he doesn't even attempt to separate the two. It suffices to point out that the two are inseparable, for the line is very thin.

Whether one has observed the Law of Moses; the traditions of the fathers or Jewish customs the consequence is the same. Thus, as Saul the man, he had advanced himself in Judaism and had even progressed *way beyond his peers*. This means that Saul had advanced himself in the study of the Law of Moses probably to the master's degree or PhD level. The Pharisees were well known for their zeal for the Law. Here is a man who is pointing out that he had advanced himself in his studies of the Law of Moses, way beyond his zealous pharisaic *peers*. Saul was a man who out ranked Pharisees of his own age group in matters of the Law of Moses!

*"though I myself have reasons for such confidence. If someone else thinks they have reasons to put confidence in the flesh, I have more: **circumcised on the eighth day,** of the people of Israel, of the tribe of Benjamin, a Hebrew of Hebrews; **in regard to the law, a Pharisee; as for zeal, persecuting the church;** as for righteousness based on the law, faultless."*
Philippians 3:4-6

On top of this illustrious career in Judaism, he had one more thing to add to that list, that set him apart from the rest of his peers. Not only was he zealous for the Law of Moses, but he also exhibited it through fiercely persecuting the Church. These were the credentials of the man Saul who persecuted the church, as far as the Law of Moses was concerned. The Faith, The Way, or the disciples stood against what Saul knew of the Law of Moses. He saw it as a nuisance that had to be stifled before it had festered with utmost urgency.

The man Saul, the Pharisee obviously knew about the importance of all the dietary laws, the Sabbath, the ten Commandments, tithes etc. He had even advanced himself in the study and strictest of adherence to these things. At some point Jesus once called out the hypocrisy of the Pharisees, how in their zeal of observing the Law, went as far as deducting tithes from spices and herbs from their backyard gardens! Saul was also one of these people who went to such great lengths in ensuring the strictest of obedience to the tithing laws.

The man was not generally acquainted with the Law of Moses; he knew it like the back of his hand. In terms of Jewish practices, he was a qualified teacher of the Law. In matters of Jewish Law, the other Apostles were probably

Saul's elementary level students. They were all novices to the Law of Moses when compared with Saul. Moreover, it was zeal for the strictest of the observance to all the above Jewish practices and more that motivated Saul in persecuting the church. He had men and women arrested to safeguard the observance of these Jewish customs.

Now this is the man whom our Lord Jesus Christ handpicked to be the Apostle to the Gentles, one who had advanced himself in Judaism. One who once persecuted believers and almost destroyed the church in its infancy because of his unwavering zeal for the Law of Moses. The same person who used to drag men and women to prison, watch with sheer satisfaction as some of them were stoned to death on account of preserving the observance of Jewish Customs.

This is the same person whom our Lord chose to send to the Gentiles instead. Why, why, why? There is no doubt that Saul was more than aware of how indispensable the Law of Moses and the Jewish customs were in the worship of YAHWEH. This reminds me of the accusations that were brought against Stephen when he was brought before the Sanhedrin and most probably Saul was one of those who plotted against him.

*'Then they secretly persuaded some men to say, "We have heard Stephen speak words of blasphemy against Moses and against God. "They produced false witnesses, who testified, "This fellow never stops speaking against this holy place and **against the law**. For we have heard him say that this Jesus of Nazareth will destroy this place and **change the customs Moses handed down to us.**" Acts 6:11,14-16'*

32

Saul and the other Jews perceived the disciples as a threat against their Jewish customs, the Law of Moses, and the worship of YAHWEH. This is the frame within which Saul viewed all disciples and their newfound beliefs. The disciples were perceived as blasphemers against Moses, God, and the Law. Because they *claimed* that Jesus of Nazareth was going to destroy the Holy temple and *was also going to change the customs that were handed down from Moses*! This is what got Saul and all the other Jews riled up. Jesus of Nazareth was going to do what? **Change the customs of Moses?** This was not going to happen under his watch! He felt that the Nazarene movement had to be crushed if its existence meant changing the customs that were handed down by Moses.

The reason why the risen Christ chose Paul to be the Apostle to the Gentiles was because of his thorough knowledge of the Law of Moses. In his infinite, omniscient wisdom, Jesus chose the man, who had devoted his entire life into studying the Law of Moses, to go and teach Gentiles about *the **Grace of God apart from that Law.*** Saul was not just zealous for the Law; he was also adept at understanding and articulating the Law as well. Therefore, I contend that there isn't even a single Gentile who may claim to possess a better understanding of the Law of Moses than Paul ever did or let alone assert that Paul did not fully comprehend just how indispensable the Law of Moses was in worship or serving God through Jesus Christ!

This was essentially the reason why Jesus sent a person who was more than qualified to teach the Law of Moses among the Jews, to go to the Gentiles instead. So that no Gentile would ever claim to possess a revelation or illumination of the Law of Moses, that would enable them to understand the said Law better than Paul ever did. No Gentile can ever claim to now understand the importance of Sabbath observance, the dietary Laws, tithing, Jewish festivals, giving, the ten Commandments in worship, better than Paul ever did!

"But when God, who set me apart from birth and called me by his grace, **was pleased to reveal his Son in me so that I might preach him among the Gentiles,** *I did not consult any man,"*
Galatians 1:15-16

As one who was given the assignment to preach to the Gentiles, the Lord had unpacked the full contents of that assignment to his messenger. Our Lord Jesus Christ revealed to Paul how the Gentiles were to worship the Father under the New Covenant. He was given the full instructions to the last detail. Paul contended that no one had taught him about the Gospel that he was preaching to the Gentiles. He was handpicked by our Lord and then sent to Gentiles. The captioned text below was a conversation that Ananias had with our Lord at Saul's conversion. This is what Jesus said about Saul, way before he sent Peter to preach at Cornelius' house.

Saul was chosen to be the Apostle to the Gentiles, long before the Jewish Christians had started preaching to uncircumcised Gentiles.

'But the Lord said to Ananias, "Go! This man is my chosen instrument to proclaim my name to the Gentiles and their kings and to the people of Israel." Acts 9:15

Our Lord Jesus chose a man who was well advanced in matters of the Law of Moses to go teach uncircumcised Gentile Christians about the righteousness of God which is by faith apart from the Law. Any given day of the week, I would rather listen to a man who was qualified in teaching the Law of Moses than a Gentile Christian who thinks he or she now understands the Law of Moses better than a former Pharisee ever did. Or a gentile Christian who thinks that they now know how to integrate the Law into Christianity better than the man who was sent by Christ to do the exact same thing for the uncircumcised Gentiles!

Chapter 4

Gentile Christians and the Law of Moses

*"Now the first Covenant **had regulations for worship**..."*
Hebrews 9:1a

It is my understanding that as uncircumcised Gentiles, we must seek to be guided by what the Apostles instructed to fellow uncircumcised Gentile Christians on what they needed to do to worship God through Christ. It really is that simple! One then wonders why some would entangle themselves in what the Circumcised Christians did in their worship of God through Christ! The New Testament writings contain all the information on what an uncircumcised Christian need to do to worship and live a life that is acceptable and pleasing to God.

From the looks of things, the entrance of the uncircumcised Gentile Christian fold into the Church was an unexpected divine phenomenon, one that was surprisingly instigated by God. As such most Jews were of the impression that Gentiles who were turning to God through Christ, should be treated like all the other Gentiles who had converted to Judaism. Despite confessing faith in Jesus as the Messiah, they still needed to add Judaism. This was largely because, the only way Gentiles could be acceptable among Jews was by converting to Judaism first, in keeping with Law of Moses.

The only problem with that presumption was the fact that these Gentiles were not converting to Judaism, but they were instead turning to God through faith in Jesus Christ. This was something new, that was unprecedented for the Jews. Even the Jewish Christians were being persecuted by fellow Jews for their newfound faith and usage of the name of Jesus of Nazareth in their worship!

*"When he arrived and **saw the evidence of the grace of God,** he was glad and encouraged them all to remain true to the Lord with all their hearts."*
Acts 11:23

I have already mentioned the circumstances that brought about the birth of the first uncircumcised Gentile Church. The Bible says that when Barnabas arrived at Antioch, "**he saw evidence of the grace of God"** among the Gentiles who had turned to Christ. After encouraging them, he then went to Tarsus in search of Paul and took him to Antioch, and together with other brethren they preached for one whole year. Trouble started when men from Judea visited the church. Their arrival coincided with the return of Paul and Barnabas, from their first missionary journey.

Upon their arrival, the brethren from Judea noticed that the Gentile Christians were not observing the Law of Moses. Kindly note that this observation came well after Paul and Barnabas had preached at Antioch for a whole year. Yet not even one of them was instructed to circumcise or observe Jewish customs or the Law of Moses!

Certain people came down from Judea to Antioch and were teaching the
believers: "Unless you are circumcised, according to the custom taught by
*Moses, **you cannot be saved**." This brought Paul and Barnabas into sharp*
dispute and debate with them. So, Paul and Barnabas were appointed,
along with some other believers, to go up to Jerusalem to see the apostles
and elders about this question.
Acts 15:1-2

What these Judeans witnessed at Antioch was unheard of,
Gentiles worshipping God without being circumcised,
observing the Law or Jewish customs! The issue only arose
because of some Circumcised Christians who were used to
the old way of converting Gentiles to Judaism through
circumcision. These men assumed that the Gentiles who
were turning to God, through Christ were also required to go
through the rites of circumcision first as the Law required.
After that, they would then start to live and worship God like
a Jew, just like all the other Jewish proselytes who had
turned to God under Judaism.

The Circumcised brothers were acting in line with what they
understood about the Law of Moses and not the New
Covenant! Their actions and motives were in agreement with
revelatory knowledge of the Old Covenant. That is why they
clashed and could not comprehend the teachings of the men,
who now possessed revelatory knowledge of the New
Covenant. What fascinated me the most was the disparity
between Barnabas' initial reaction when he first arrived at
Antioch and that of the men from Judea.

The scriptures reveal that Barnabas *"saw the evidence of the*
grace of God" among the uncircumcised Gentile Christians and

that was enough for him. What was it that Barnabas saw that the Circumcised brothers from Judea didn't? The *'evidence of the grace of God'*. According to Barnabas, the indication of true worship was the *'evidence of the grace of God'*. He saw that God was already at work in the lives of these believers, albeit that they were not circumcised or observing Jewish customs in their lifestyle or public worship. This is something that only a person who possessed revelatory knowledge of the New Covenant would understand.

As for the Judean Christians who did not possess this understanding, true signs of worship were circumcision, observing the Law and Jewish customs! Barnabas and the Judean Christians were operating on two different plains! *The former saw grace while the latter perceived absence of the Law and **therefore failed to comprehend grace**!* Does one grasp the consequence of emphasizing Law over grace? This merely implies that the brothers from Judea judged the Uncircumcised believers' worship and lifestyle by standards of the Old Covenant and not the New!

The text captioned above reveals that the Old Covenant, had regulations for worship, these were some of the regulations that they felt the uncircumcised Gentile Christians must observe, for their worship to be proper. In essence the men from Judea intimated that these Gentiles were worshipping and serving God the wrong way, the correct way was to keep or observe the Law of Moses starting with circumcision for them to be acceptable to God. The issue had more to do with how they served and worshipped God after salvation. Yes, they had believed, repented, and even received the Holy Spirit, but they also needed circumcision and to observe the Law for them to *properly* worship God. This was the proper way of doing things according to the Law and Jewish custom!

As mentioned above, these men were being motivated by what they understood about the Law of Moses rather than what they understood about Christ and what he had done at Cavalry. From a Jewish Law perspective, the men of Judea were correct, yet from a New Covenant perspective in terms of Gentile Christian worship, they were gravely mistaken. That's why Paul and Barnabas objected to their teachings. God had already shown signs that he had accepted Gentile worship without the Law of Moses by giving them the Holy Spirit. Hence all those regulations from the first Covenant had fallen away that determined acceptability before God, as God had already accepted the uncircumcised believers.

Paul and Barnabas were the first people to object to this kind of teaching which was not motivated from one's understanding of the redeeming work of Christ. They more than objected to this teaching that Gentile Christians should keep the Law of Moses or observe Jewish customs to please God. According to their understanding Judaism was an abstract entity of no relevance to Gentile Christians. Therefore, the matter was then taken up to Jerusalem. The matter that had to be determined, was what needed to be done with the **uncircumcised-Gentiles** turning to God **through Christ**.

Initially, the subject matter that brought about the Council of Jerusalem, was Circumcision. But after a report had been given about what the Holy Spirit was doing among the Gentiles, some believers who belonged to the Pharisee camp, stood up and immediately recommended that the Gentile believers must be circumcised and required to observe the Law of Moses!

> "Then some of the believers who belonged to the party of the Pharisees stood up and said, "The Gentiles must be circumcised and required to obey the law of Moses." **The apostles and elders met to consider this question.**"
> Acts 15:5-6

This is what the Apostles and the Elders had to consider; they met to consider this question. **Should the Gentile believers be Circumcised and observe the Law of Moses in their worship and lifestyle?** The scriptures are very clear on this! The question of whether or not the uncircumcised Gentiles were in fact "believers" was never raised. They had in fact believed in Jesus and the whole Church regarded them as believers. After much discussion, Peter got up and addressed them:

> "Brothers, you know that some time ago God made a choice among you that the Gentiles might hear from my lips the message of the gospel and believe. God, who knows the heart, **showed that he accepted them by giving the Holy Spirit to them,** just as he did to us. **He did not discriminate between us and them,** for he purified their hearts by faith."
> Acts15:7-8

Peter began by first recounting what had happened earlier when Our Lord had sent him to preach to Cornelius, an uncircumcised Gentile, and his whole household. That is how we finally grasp the full significance of that incident and how it helped in shaping the Gentile Christian theology. Record shows that he was the Apostle to the Jews but at one point the Lord had appeared and instructed him to go to the house of Cornelius an uncircumcised Gentile. This incident rocked his Jewish mind to the core. What happened at Cornelius' house was quite disturbing indeed.

Even the Gentiles who did not have God's Law, the uncircumcised, swine eaters and Sabbath desecraters had received the Holy Spirit of God, just like they had done! God did not place a distinction between the Jews and Gentiles when he gave them the Holy Spirit, even though the latter did not have God's Law. Peter then intimated that the Law of Moses was a burden that only the Jews had to carry. *"we and our forefathers."* Meaning that even though they (Jewish Christians) had been saved through faith in Jesus, they were still subject to the Law of Moses.

According to Peter, this whole experience revealed this truth; the burden of keeping the Law of Moses was for all the Jews or circumcised Christians only and not uncircumcised Gentiles turning to God through faith in the Lord Jesus Christ. Secondly, he pointed out the *primary* reason why Gentile Christians should not be subjected to the Law of Moses. The Jews felt that for Gentile worship to be *acceptable* before God, they must be circumcised and then observe the Law of Moses, or in other words live and worship God like the Jews. Peter's response specifically addresses this concern.

*"God who knows the heart, **has shown us that he has accepted Gentiles by giving them the Holy Spirit**, just as he did to us. He did not discriminate between us and them, **he purified their hearts by faith."***
Acts 15:7-8

Peter assured his peers that, if at all they were indeed worried that God would not be pleased or accept the Gentiles, if they were to worship Him without observing the Law of Moses, or the Jewish customs. God had shown all the Jews, that He had already ***accepted*** these uncircumcised Gentiles by giving them the Holy Spirit. Whatever concerns that they had, God had already settled them. While they were concerned that God would not accept the Gentiles or that what they were doing was unacceptable before God. Whereas, God had already accepted the uncircumcised believers, He had manifested or communicated his acceptance by giving them the Holy Spirit!

In all this, Peter was merely informing his Jewish counterparts that, uncircumcised Gentile Christians do not need to worship God the Jewish way for their worship to be acceptable before God. According to the Jewish school of thought, whoever does not worship God the Jewish way in keeping with Law of Moses and the Jewish traditions, is completely unacceptable before God. That is the exact ideology that they wanted to foster among the Gentiles. On the contrary, through the guidance and revelation of the Holy Spirit, God said no to this. This ideology is not true or consistent with the Gospel.

Before Peter spoke up, it appeared as though the decision to subject Gentiles under the Law of Moses was almost unanimous among the Jewish Christians present. Peter objected to this and issued a solemn warning *"Now then, **why do you try to test God** by putting on the necks of the believers a yoke that neither we nor our ancestors have been able to bear? No!"* (Acts15v10). He warned that in trying to impose the Jewish customs or Jewish Law onto the Gentile Christians, they were in fact not *serving God but putting God to the test.* The Gentiles do not **need** to worship or do anything the Jewish way for them or whatever they do to be acceptable before God through Christ. Whoever does this, would be putting God to the test or challenging God.

Do we really grasp the connotations of Peter's chilling rebuke? We need to realise that it is God who decided to accept uncircumcised Gentiles and gave them instructions on how they may worship Him apart from the Law! It is God who decided to give them the Holy Spirit as a sign of acceptance. Peter implied that **whoever** tries to impose the Law of Moses on uncircumcised believers would be challenging God. *This would be like telling God that he made a mistake by accepting uncircumcised believers and allowing them to worship Him without observing the Law of Moses and Jewish customs!*

The actual reality was simply that, the way the Gentile Christians were worshipping and serving God without the Law of Moses was offensive and unacceptable to the Jews! All this pressure of needing to subject Gentiles to the Law of

Moses had more to do with Jewish attitude towards uncircumcised Gentiles, rather than God! Then James also chipped in who by the way, was known to be a devout Jewish Christian who had high regard of the Law, but this is what he had to say on the matter.

*"Simon has described to us how **God first intervened** to choose a people for his name from the Gentiles..."* **Acts 15:14**

According to James, it was God who had intervened and decided to choose a people for his name among the Gentiles. It was God who initiated this move of grafting uncircumcised Gentiles to his fold. He therefore was the only one who best understood what should be done with these Gentiles. The whole council at Jerusalem concurred with Paul and Barnabas' position that all the Gentiles were not to be subjected to the Law of Moses *in anyway*. Thus, for us to understand how this determination affects all of us today. We must ask ourselves, why was that council held in the first place?

The content of the letter that was written to the Gentile churches does confirm that indeed the matters that were deliberated upon at the Council had less to do with Salvation but more to do with matters of practical holiness. What the uncircumcised Gentiles had to do to live a holy life in Jesus Christ. The matter of whether Gentiles are to keep the Law after salvation was settled there and then, a long time ago! This is what the Apostolic council instructed. After salvation they would fare very well in the Lord to avoid all these things.

*"It seemed good to the **Holy Spirit** and to us **not to burden you with anything beyond the following requirements**: You are to abstain from food sacrificed to idols, from blood, from the meat of strangled animals and from sexual immorality. **You will do well to avoid these things. Farewell.**" Acts 15:28-29*

A very similar issue later came up again on Paul's return to Jerusalem towards the end of his ministry before his eventual arrest in Acts 21. The Jewish Christians or at least the leadership at Jerusalem had no problems whatsoever with Paul in as far as his teaching to the Gentiles were concerned. They expressed no dissatisfaction with the fact that Paul was teaching Gentile Christians to disregard the Law of Moses, circumcision and living according to Jewish customs.

This was the correct doctrinal position in as far as Gentile worship was concerned and was well in line with the determination that was given by the earlier Church council. To show that this was indeed the correct doctrinal position, the Church Leadership issued out a second letter and dispatched it to all the Gentile Churches, reaffirming the earlier position. It is noteworthy that, even though they were zealous for the Law and their Jewish customs, their earlier doctrinal position so far as the Gentile Christians were concerned, had not changed. As a way of mitigating the situation, James informed Paul that they had written to the Gentiles reinforcing their earlier position.

*"**As for the Gentile believers**, we have written to them our decision that they should abstain from food sacrificed to idols, from blood, from the meat of strangled animals and from sexual immorality."*
Acts 21:25

46

This was close to fifteen to twenty or more years after the council of Jerusalem and yet the doctrinal position for the Gentile Christians had not yet changed. The only crisis that they sought to remedy was what Paul was presumably teaching Jewish Christians living in Gentile territory. As for the uncircumcised Gentiles, the Jerusalem Leadership merely reinforced the earlier instruction verbatim! Interesting... Here a very distinct line in the sand was drawn between Gentile and Jewish Christianity. The doctrinal position is now much more pronounced.

Jewish Christians everywhere were then instructed to continue regarding the Law of Moses, circumcising their children and continue to live according to Jewish customs. As for the Gentiles, they were never required to regard the Law of Moses and to live according to Jewish customs. This then concludes the matter on whether or not the two covenants overlap. There appears to be a Covenantal overlap in as far as Jewish Christians were concerned and not the uncircumcised Gentiles. Uncircumcised believers were exclusively grafted onto the New Covenant and not the Old.

Moreover, our worship as uncircumcised believers is regulated by the instructions and commandments from the Apostles, specifically to Gentile believers. God accommodated and grafted us onto the New Covenant and not the Old! We are saved by grace through faith in our Lord Jesus so that we may worship God under the New Covenant. At the earlier council, the Church leadership distanced itself from the circumcised Christians who were going around teaching the believers to circumcise and observe the Law of Moses. This is what the Church Leadership had to say to the Gentile Church on such people.

*"We have heard that **some went out from us without our authorization** and **disturbed** you, **troubling your minds by what they say**."*
Act 15:24

The Church leadership of Jerusalem informed all the Gentile Churches to disregard or ignore any teachings that were being peddled by some Circumcised Christians among them. The Church declared that these men who were troubling them by trying to subject them to the Law of Moses, were acting out of their own enterprise. The Church had not authorized them to teach such teachings among the Gentile believers. Whatever they were teaching was not authorized by the Apostles or did not come from Christ.

The Church then sent Judas and Silas together with Paul, Barnabas, and their delegation so that they could confirm all this through the word of mouth. Thus, through the authority and revelatory knowledge from the Holy Spirit, the Jewish Christian leadership did not subject Gentile Christians to the Law of Moses. Despite the fact that they were very zealous for the Law and had instructed fellow Jewish Christians living among the Gentiles to uphold the Law of Moses and Jewish Customs. They did not give such an instruction to the Gentile Churches or Christians. They also instructed Gentiles not to pay attention to men who tried doing so, for these people had no authority from anyone to teach those things!

Chapter 5

What is the Gospel of Christ?

"I am astonished that you are so quickly deserting the one who called you by the grace of Christ and are turning to a different gospel--which is really no gospel at all. Evidently some people are throwing you into confusion and are trying to pervert the gospel of Christ."
Galatians 1:6-7

Now that we understand that there were two distinct groups of Christians under the Early New Testament Church: Circumcised and uncircumcised Christians. Consequently, we are now better placed to determine the true Gospel of Christ to the uncircumcised Christians. This is only possible if we are cognizant of the fact that there are two Gospels that are found within the New Testament writings. The general understanding of the Gospel among many, is simply *"the Good News of Christ"*. Nevertheless, it is my understanding that Gospel also implies *"a set of instructions or teachings on how one may be saved and then live for Christ after salvation."*

Thus, by pointing out the existence of two Gospels within the New Testament writings, this implies that there exists the Gospel to the circumcised believers and then the Gospel to the Gentile Christians. The first Gospel, the Gospel to the Circumcised, contained a set of instructions and teachings on how they may be saved and then live for God through faith in

Jesus Christ. Then the second Gospel, the Gospel to the uncircumcised believers, contains a set of instructions on how they could be saved and then worship and live for God through faith in Jesus Christ. As already alluded to in previous chapters, the difference arose because Circumcised Christians were required to uphold the Law of Moses and observe Jewish customs for the simple reason that they were Jews or circumcised, while uncircumcised Gentiles were not required to do any of those things by God.

*"To the Jews I became like a Jew, to win the Jews. To those under the law I became like one under the law (though I myself am not under the law), so as to win those under the law. To those not having the law I became like one not having the law (**though I am not free from God's law but am under Christ's law**), so as to win those not having the law."*
1 Corinthians 9:20-21

This was largely because Circumcised Christians could not worship God or live like Gentiles even after confessing Jesus as their Savior. Whereas Gentile Christians who were turning to God through Christ, were likewise, not required to worship God and live like the Jews or the circumcised. It is failure to appreciate this distinction that has led us to where we are today. It's incumbent upon all of us to determine which set of instructions under the New Testament writings, were written specifically to a Jewish Christian audience and which set of instructions were given to the Gentile Christians.

As uncircumcised Christians, we are bound to the Gospel for the Gentiles. Meaning our worship and lifestyle must be predicated upon the instructions of the Apostles to the Gentile Christians in particular. Aforementioned, is the fact that the Apostle who was given the teachings or instructions for Gentile worship through direct revelation from our Lord Jesus Christ was Paul.

> "It seemed good **to the Holy Spirit and to us** not to burden you with anything beyond the following requirements..." Acts 15:28

While it is true that the Apostles through the inspiration of the Holy Spirit, agreed that Gentile Christians should not be subjected to the Law of Moses, it was the Apostle Paul who was given the direct revelation of Gentile worship. Everything, all the nuances of worship that the Gentiles needed to know in order to worship and live for God through faith in Jesus Christ was revealed to Paul. The Lord Jesus through his chosen Apostle, gave express instructions on how Gentiles may worship God without observing the Law of Moses or Jewish customs.

> "I want you to know, brothers, that the **gospel I preached** is not something that man made up. I did not receive it from any man, nor was I taught it; rather, **I received it by revelation from Jesus Christ.**"
> Galatians 1:11-12

The Apostles had exclusive right and authority in terms of Christian doctrine in general. Paul then revealed that he had exclusive authority in terms of Gentile Christian doctrine because of the grace of God that was upon him.

> "Now, brothers, I want to remind you of the **gospel I preached to you,** which you received and on which you have taken your stand. By **this gospel you are saved**, if you hold firmly to the **word I preached to you**. Otherwise, you have believed in vain." 1Corinth 15:1-2

Evidently, the Apostle was being exclusive here. He informed the Gentile Christians at Corinth that they attain and maintain salvation by holding on firmly to the instructions that he had given them! Paul did not put a *"we"* here. He was emphatic in his declaration that it is what he taught that they should receive and take a stand on, in their walk of faith. Failure to do so meant that they would have believed in vain! This indicates that as Gentile Christians, we are saved and maintain that salvation by holding on and adhering to Paul's Gospel! The very same Gospel that no man had taught him and received by direct revelation from Christ.

> *"I went in response to a revelation and, meeting privately with those esteemed as leaders, **I presented to them the gospel that I preach among the Gentiles**. I wanted to be sure I was not running and had not been running my race in vain." Galatians 2:2*

Paul also revealed to the Galatians that, he went to Jerusalem, met the Apostles privately and presented his gospel/teaching to the Gentiles. This reveals that the Apostles were all aware of what Paul was teaching among the Gentiles. He had made that certain by personally going to Jerusalem, specifically for that purpose.

> *"As for those who were held in high esteem—whatever they were makes no difference to me; God does not show favoritism— **they added nothing to my message**. On the contrary, they recognized that I had been entrusted with the task of preaching the gospel to the uncircumcised, just as Peter had been to the circumcised." Galatians 2:6-7*

Here, Paul reveals that after he had presented his gospel, the 'esteemed' Apostles did not object, add or subtract anything from his teaching. They more than agreed with his teaching, and also recognized that Paul is the one who had indeed been entrusted by our Lord Jesus with the *task* of *preaching the gospel* to the uncircumcised just as Peter had been to the Circumcised. This task wasn't just preaching but laying down the doctrinal foundation for all uncircumcised Gentile Christian worship. This task was given to Paul from above and the 'esteemed' Apostles had recognized it!

"James, Peter and John, those esteemed as pillars, gave me and Barnabas the right hand of fellowship when they recognized the grace given to me. ***They agreed that we should go to the Gentiles****, and they to the circumcised." Galatians 2:8-9*

James, Peter, and John the most respected among the Apostles had consented and approved of Paul's teaching or gospel to the Gentiles. These three recognized the grace of God that was upon Paul, hence they resolved that Paul should go and teach the Gentiles about how to live and worship God through faith in Jesus. Paul's gospel or teaching covered all areas of life that concerns an uncircumcised believer. This gospel covered all aspects of Christian living, from salvation, worship, serving God, marriage, family life, daily life, giving, life after death, gifts of the Holy Spirit, Pastoring, appointment of leaders in Church etc.

Paul gave instructions on every aspect of a believer's life, which instructions he generally referred to as *'my gospel'*. It must also be noted that Paul's letters were occasional, they were meant to address certain issues that arose in matters of Gentile Christian doctrine. There were so many 'Circumcised' Christians who went around Gentile Churches challenging

Paul's teachings (gospel) and tried to introduce their own teachings (gospels) on Christianity.

Therefore, Paul had to inform his uncircumcised believers' audience from the different churches that, they are saved for as long as they believe and remained in his teachings; that he received the teachings by direct revelation and that *He had taught them all there is to know about living a life that pleases God* (1Thess.4:1-2). This shows that Jesus revealed to Paul everything about uncircumcised Gentile worship. If we want to know anything about salvation we must believe and hold on to what Apostle Paul taught. If we want to know anything about pleasing God as uncircumcised Gentile Christians, we must pay attention to what Apostle Paul taught.

In fact, in any matter that concerns an uncircumcised Gentile Christian, it is what the Apostle Paul instructed that has authority. *"By this gospel you are saved, if you hold firmly to the word I preached to you"*. This instruction is pretty much exclusive and authoritative, we must hold firmly to the word that Apostle Paul preached. Any teaching that is not derived from the express instructions from the Apostles to the Gentile church but is predicated upon the Law of Moses or Jewish customs, is a perversion of the True Gospel of Jesus Christ.

Sabbath observance, exclusive use of the name of Jehovah in worship and witnessing, dietary laws, religious festivals, Ten Commandments observance, tithing of any kind, prosperity gospel, building money alters, spiritual fathers or back to sender, and the prophetic movement. If all these practices cannot be solely established or derived upon the express teachings of the Apostles to the Gentile Church, their practice or observance is a perversion of the True Gospel of Jesus Christ.

It is against this background that we must then understand the proper context of Paul's epistle to the Galatians. Paul declared that there were some men who were trying to pervert the **Gospel of Christ** by teaching the Galatians a new set of different instructions on how they may be saved and please God after salvation. A different Gospel in this sense, merely stands for teachings or instructions that did not come from Christ to the church through his Apostles or through the revelation of the New Covenant.

The Apostle went as far as contending that whatever these men were teaching, was not in fact the Gospel of Christ or the teachings of Christ to the **Gentile Church**. Paul began by pointing out that whatever these men were teaching was *no gospel at all*, because their teachings did not come from Christ. He even intimated that anyone who teaches Gentile Christians a different teaching or gives them different instructions on salvation and righteousness, from the ones that they (the Apostles) had given them, such a man or even an angel stands eternally condemned by God.

In other words, Paul instructed the Gentiles not to entertain anyone, not even an angel from above or even he and the other Apostles, if they came back teaching or giving them different instructions on salvation and righteousness, from the ones they first gave them! According to Paul's expert opinion whatever these men were teaching, threw the whole church into confusion! This just reveals the massive impact that whatever these men were teaching had on the whole church! It cast some doubt on the veracity of what the Apostle had taught about salvation and living for Christ!

*"I am astonished that you are so quickly deserting the one who called you by the grace of Christ and are turning to a different gospel-- **which is really no gospel at all**. Evidently some people are throwing you into confusion and are trying to **pervert the gospel of Christ**. But even if we or an angel from heaven should preach a gospel other than the one we preached to you, let him be eternally condemned!"*
Galatians 1:6-8

It has been widely accepted that the men whom Paul was denouncing here were Jews, but I am fully persuaded to believe otherwise. I am convinced that these men were probably circumcised-Gentile Christians who had initially converted to Judaism and then later became Christians. These were circumcised Gentiles who were already living and worshipping God like the Jews. Something they probably retained even after converting to Christianity. The mere fact that these men made such great inroads and managed to convince so many Gentiles to submit to their teachings, gives the Jewish-proselyte-Christian theory great plausibility.

As mentioned in previous chapters, Jewish proselytes were also present in Jerusalem at the feast of Pentecost. Philip preached or witnessed to an Ethiopian Eunuch, who evidently was already a convert to Judaism, who then became a Christian. It is probably this group of Christians that brought about all the controversy in the Gentile Church. This was also largely because Jewish proselytizing was a common phenomenon throughout the Roman Empire or Gentile territory.

> *"For there are many **rebellious** people, full of meaningless talk and deception, **especially those of the circumcision group. They must be silenced**, because they are disrupting whole households **by teaching things they ought not to teach**—and that for the sake of dishonest gain. This saying is true. Therefore rebuke them sharply, so that they will **be sound in the faith and will pay no attention to Jewish myths or to the merely human commands** of those who reject the truth."*
> Titus 1:10-14

I wish to bring it to your attention that it was these Jewish-proselyte-Christians or the circumcised Gentiles who rejected Paul's teachings to the Gentiles and even casted aspersions on his Apostleship. Their resentment had more to do with what they understood about the Law of Moses than what they knew or understood about the glory of Christ and his redemptive work at cavalry. In fact, these men were trying to force the Gentile Christians to worship God and live like Jews. Paul's letter was a rebuttal to the teachings(gospel) that were being propagated by these men.

It appears that the Galatians were being taught that they needed to observe the Law of Moses to attain salvation(2:21); perfection in Christ (3:4); that they were under God's curse for not observing the Law(3:10) that they needed to Circumcise in order to attain the blessing of Abraham (3:13-15); that they should observe special days or Sabbaths, new moon celebrations as well as other annual or seasonal feasts or festivals on the Jewish calendar (4:10) among many other things from the Law of Moses. The confusion that Paul mentioned earlier, emanated from the fact that all these things that they were teaching are all in the Bible. Moreover, these were things that the Circumcised Christians observed both in their lifestyle and in worship!

If the Apostles in Jerusalem had allowed the Circumcised Christians to observe these commandments or regulation in their lifestyle and worship, why didn't Paul also teach them to do the same? Weren't these commandments given to all of God's people of all time, Jews, and Gentile alike? Isn't it that faith in Jesus qualified them to be a people of God? The most biblical and spiritual conclusion was that Gentile Christians must also observe God's commandments and Jewish traditions with the intention of pleasing God or at least attain perfection in Christ.

They too needed circumcision for them to receive the blessing of Abraham and assert full rights to be numbered among God's people in line with the requirements of the Law. I presume these were some of the arguments using scriptural references that these men had presented to buttress their claims. It is this desire to attain perfection and blessings that lured some of the Gentile believers away from the true gospel. The Uncircumcised Christians were led to believe that they needed to observe the Law of Moses to attain perfection in Christ or to fully please God or to be blessed by God!

Interestingly enough, it appears as though the prevailing assumption among many today is that; If a Church denomination or a Pastor is preaching what the Apostles instructed on salvation then this indicates that they would be teaching the true gospel of Christ. Whatever the Pastor teaches on what believers must do to then worship or please God does not pervert the gospel. However, this position isn't accurate in as far as the true gospel of Christ is concerned.

Whatever the Church denomination or Pastor teaches on salvation and practical holiness must be solely predicated upon the express teachings from the Apostles to the Gentile Church. One may indeed pervert the gospel either by what they teach on what sinners need to do to attain salvation or what they teach on what believers need to do, to then worship and please the Lord. This is why Paul said that you attain and maintain salvation by holding on to my teaching (gospel).

Peter warned his fellow Jewish brethren 'not to put God to the test' by subjecting uncircumcised believers to the Law. Paul declared that all those who introduce a new teaching on any subject other than the ones they gave to the Gentiles stands 'eternally condemned by God'. He also warned all Gentile believers who had given in to this perverted gospel or new teachings on Christianity that "they had been cut-off from grace and alienated from Christ". (Galatians 6:1-5)

Chapter 6

How and Why was the Law abolished?

"The Law was abolished so that we may become acceptable or righteous before God through what Christ did on the Cross and not what was written in the Law of Moses."

In our pursuit of understanding the New Testament, we must tackle the usage and interpretation of the Law under the Gentile Church of Christ. Much of the perversion and distortion of the True Gospel came because of the misplacement of the truth of God in the Old Testament Scriptures under the New Testament Gentile Church. To clearly decipher how scriptures from the Old Testament can apply in our lives today. They must be approached with the full realization that they were written for the Jews who lived and worshipped God under **a *different truth of God*.**

Contained therein, is the truth of God that applied to people who were exclusively bound to the Old Covenant, that was upheld by observing the Law. We on the other hand are a different audience living under *a **new truth.*** Currently, the truth of God is that God now accepts uncircumcised Gentiles to worship him through Christ under a different Covenant! We are now bound to God through the New Covenant, so we don't need the Law of Moses to uphold this Covenant!

This indicates that we are not required to do what the Jews had to do for them to please God. All this came about through the death of our Lord Jesus Christ. Already mentioned is the fact that, Paul received direct revelation of Gentile worship, as such he was the one who instructed all Gentiles that the Law of Moses was abolished through the death of Christ. One may go through all the other Apostolic writings from Peter, James, John or even Matthew, and see if they can find texts that say that the Law of Moses was abolished by the death of Christ.

The Apostle further explains that it was the death of Christ that abolished the Law of Moses and absolved all Gentiles of the requirement to observe it both in our worship and lifestyle. While the other Apostles understood that Gentile Christians could not be subjected to the law of Moses, the Apostle Paul as one who possessed the full revelation of Gentile worship, then gave instructions on how this could be done! The circumcised Christians were all befuddled by this new development as they could not even begin to fathom how a person could actually please God without the Law of Moses!

Surprisingly, the prevailing belief in Christian circles today is that Jesus's death on the cross abolished *only* the *ceremonial parts* of the Law of Moses. However, this belief is not predicated upon the teachings from the Apostle, but upon the perversions on the gospel, that have been introduced under the Gentile Church. To justify usage of commands from the Law of Moses or Jewish customs under uncircumcised

Gentile worship, people have now altered the implications of the death of Christ on the Mosaic Law!

Some have now categorized the Law of Moses into two parts, the *"ceremonial"* and *"moral"* law. They assert that the ceremonial law is the part of the Law that governed the sacrificial system, the religious festivals and or dietary laws depending on church denomination! As such, that is the part of the Law that Jesus abolished, hence they then contend that Gentile Christians are still obligated to observe the moral part of the Law of Moses. They then categorize whatever they want the believers to observe as being part of the moral Law!

However, this distinction of the Law into Moral and Ceremonial Law is found nowhere in the Bible, it's something that is of a purely human construct as the following reference can confirm.

> *"The division of the Jewish law into different categories **is a human construct** designed to better understand the nature of God and **define which laws church-age Christians are still required to follow**. Many believe the ceremonial law is not applicable, but we are bound by the Ten Commandments. All the law is useful for instruction (2 Timothy 3:16), and nothing in the Bible indicates that God intended a distinction of categories."*
> https://www.gotquestions.org/ceremonial-law.html

As the above quote can reveal, separation of the Law into Ceremonial and Moral Law is not Biblical, it is a heretical practice under the Gentile Christian Church. Whoever thought of making such a distinction of the Law into Moral and Ceremonial Law so as to **define** which commands from the Law of Moses are still applicable to the Church was gravely mistaken. This whole issue or question was settled at the council of Jerusalem by the Apostles as mentioned in the previous Chapters. That Church council is very much definitive because all the influential Apostles were present Peter, James, John, Barnabas, and Paul. No one other than these Apostles has the authority to make such a determination.

There was no need for Gentiles, some centuries later, to forego the resolution passed by the Apostles. To then try to determine or define which commands from the Law of Moses are still applicable under the Gentile Christian Church. This whole confusion came from observing the Jewish Christians in the book of Acts and some teachings in the gospels. The mere fact that Jewish Christians continued to observe the Law of Moses or some parts of the Law is no indication that all uncircumcised Gentile Christians must also do the same!

It is also quite remarkable to note that the same people who make such claims, that Jesus only abolished the so called *"ceremonial Law"*. When called upon why they insist on strict obedience to some parts of the Law of Moses, they turn to Matthew 5! Using this text, they vainly try to justify their theological bias of using some parts of the Law because Jesus said that he did not come to abolish the Law but to *fulfill* it! Again, this does not make much sense at all. Here's why.

So, according to their understanding, Jesus only abolished *"the ceremonial part"* of the Law and at the same time He did not come to abolish the Law but came to fulfill it? The reason why all this doesn't make much sense at all is because the same text expressly mentions that not even an iota from the Law will pass away. There is no mention of the *'ceremonial Law'* being abolished in this text. On the contrary, this text points out that everything (even the smallest letter, commas, or periods) contained in the Law shall not be abolished!

> *"**Do not think that I have come to abolish the Law** or the Prophets; I have **not come to abolish them but to fulfill them**. I tell you the truth, until heaven and earth disappear, **not the smallest letter, not the least stroke of a pen**, will by any means disappear from the Law until everything is accomplished." Matthew 5:17-18*

As I have already mentioned, the gospel of Matthew was written to a Jewish Christian audience. I have also revealed that the Jewish Christians were very zealous for the Law of Moses. The message and tone in the gospel of Matthew confirms this biblical and historical fact. This gospel was written to Jewish Christians who continued to observe the Law of Moses even after Pentecost. Even this discourse or teachings by Jesus is referred to as the sermon on the Mount which is more of a sequel to Mt Sinai!

Need I constantly remind that Apostle Peter particularly warned his Jewish brethren against subjecting Gentiles to the Law of Moses. He told them that the burden of observing the Law was theirs to bear as Jews! This then essentially corroborates the fact that this text In Matthew does not apply to uncircumcised Gentile Christians. Some of the teachings in the Gospels must be understood from a Jewish Christian perspective.

Paul, the Apostle, as one who was endowed with the revelation of the gospel to the Gentiles fully elucidated on why Gentile Christians are not required to keep the Law of Moses or to worship God through Jesus Christ the Jewish way. Paul explained that Jesus abolished the Law of Moses for us Gentiles. When making and stressing this point, Paul never used the term *"fulfill"*, he used such definitive words like **"abolished"** **"end"** or **"cancelled"**. So, it's very clear what he meant by using such terms. The Law of Moses was abolished because it was hostile to all uncircumcised Gentiles.

James at the Council of Jerusalem opined that *"God first intervened to choose a people for his name from the Gentiles"* It was, therefore, God who had taken this initiative and chose to accommodate uncircumcised Gentiles. He then gave Paul the full revelation as to how he was going to do so. For Him to do that, God had to abolish the Old Covenant first, so that he could accept Gentiles through faith in His Son Jesus Christ of Nazareth under the *New Covenant*.

"by abolishing in his flesh, the law with its commandments and regulations…"
Ephesians 2:16

Here the Apostle expounded on the reason why the Law was abolished for us Gentiles. He explains that Jesus **abolished** the Law with **its** *commandments and regulations* through his **body**. He did this through the cross by which he put to death or an end to the Law. Notice that Paul said that Jesus abolished *the Law with its commandments and regulations*. The Apostle did not say that Jesus only abolished **some parts of** the Law with its commandments and regulations. The term Law is a *compound* term because it was made up of commandments and regulations. Paul was referring to the wholesome thing, The Law with **its** *"commandments and regulations"*. This meant that every commandment and regulation that was given under that Law was abolished when the "Law" was abolished. The whole *content* of the Law was abolished and not just parts of it.

> *"When you were dead in your sins and in the uncircumcision of your sinful nature, God made you alive with Christ. He forgave us all our sins, **having canceled the written code, with its regulations,** that was against us and that stood opposed to us; **he took it away, nailing it to the cross."***
> Colossians 2: 13-14

While addressing another Gentile Church, the Colossians, who were also being pressured to observe the Law of Moses and Jewish customs. He revealed that, first Jesus cancelled the **written code** or the Law, **with its regulations and** He did so by taking it away and nailing it to the cross!

> *"But now, by dying to what once bound us, we have been released from **the law** so that we serve in the **new way of the Spirit**, and not in the old way of **the written code."** Romans 7:6*

To the Romans he then uses the terms *"law"* and *"written code"* interchangeably in the same sentence or verse. This clearly indicates that the Apostle always used these words interchangeably, but they meant the same thing. Here too, Paul was talking about the Law of Moses and what God had done to it for Gentiles to be acceptable in worship. In my own words: The *Law was abolished so that we may become acceptable before God, through what Christ did on the Cross and not what was written in the Law of Moses.* Before the death of Christ, one was regarded unacceptable before God because of what was written in the Law. Now because of Christ, everything has now changed. *Even Gentiles who do not observe the Law are now acceptable before God because of what Christ did.* This is a very simple gospel truth that has eluded many!

All this implied that the commands and regulations under the Law do not regulate Gentile Christian worship. That was why Paul had to instruct the uncircumcised believers at Colossae, not to allow anyone to judge their walk of faith in Christ, using the Law. We are now liable if not accountable to God through a different Covenant, agreement, or standard of worship. This new Covenant is also now maintained and upheld by observing and keeping the instructions from the Apostles to the Gentiles!

> *"Therefore do not let anyone judge you by what you eat or drink, or with regard to a religious festival, a New Moon celebration or a Sabbath day. These are a shadow of the things that were to come; the reality, however, is found in Christ." Colossians 2:16-17*

There is now a **new** *form of righteousness* which is a new reality that is synonymous with the New Covenant. The Law was superseded or abrogated by the *Law of Christ.* When God abolished the Old Covenant, he established the New Covenant. All uncircumcised Christians are now accommodated under the New Covenant. Jesus gave the terms and conditions of this Covenant through his Apostles on how we may please or worship the Father. The bulk of the New Testament writings were written specifically to uncircumcised believers. They gave full instructions on how Gentile Christians must worship God. It is these instructions that now sanctify and regulate our worship. We now please God and uphold the New Covenant by what the Apostles instructed.

*"Finally, brothers, we **instructed** you how to live in order **to please God**, as in fact you are living. Now we ask you and urge you in the Lord Jesus to do this more and more. For you know **what commandments we gave you by the authority of the Lord Jesus.** 1Thessalonians 4:1-2*

*""... because of the grace God gave me to be a minister of Christ Jesus to the Gentiles. He gave me the ministry of proclaiming the gospel of God, so that the Gentiles might become an **offering acceptable to God, sanctified by the Holy Spirit**.*
*Therefore, I glory in Christ Jesus in my service to God I will not venture to speak anything except what Christ has accomplished through me **in leading the Gentiles to obey God** by what I have said and done"*
Romans 15:15-18

To the Romans, Paul also revealed three things that his ministry was fostered on; firstly, ensuring that all the Gentiles may become acceptable before God; secondly, that the Gentiles are sanctified by the Holy Spirit; and lastly, that Christ was now leading the Gentiles to obey God by what he (Paul) said or did! This last statement shouldn't be taken lightly and must be given the attention it deserves. Christ determined that Gentiles can now obey God through what Paul commanded!

*"If anybody thinks he is a prophet or spiritually gifted, let him acknowledge that **what I am writing to you is the Lord's command**." 1Corinth 14:37*

*To the married **I give this command (not I, but the Lord):** A wife must not separate from her husband. 1Corinth 7:10*

The folly of the Jews...

*"Since they did not know the righteousness that comes from God and sought to establish their own, they did not submit to God's righteousness. **Christ is the end of the law so that there may be righteousness for everyone who believes**." Romans 10:3-4*

Paul pinpointed the folly of the Jews, that they didn't know about the righteousness that comes from God by faith. They were only aware of the righteousness that came through strictly observing the Law of Moses and that's the one they zealously sought to establish. He then boldly declared that *"Christ is the end of the Law, so that there may be righteousness for everyone who believes."* He first revealed that his fellow Israelites were very zealous for the Law of Moses, but their zeal was not predicated on knowledge of the New Covenant! Now because of what Christ did, the righteousness of God Is for everyone who *believes*.

All that you need is *belief for you* to attain and maintain this righteousness. Please note, that salvation or this righteousness that we attain through faith does not qualify us to observe the Law of Moses. The Law was the means by which people upheld the Old Covenant.

In a nutshell, God abolished the Old Covenant in order to establish the New! (Hebrews 8v13) So that we may worship and please him through the New Covenant.

Chapter 7

Pentecostal Churches in light of the True Gospel

"Why do you look at the speck of sawdust in your brother's eye and pay no attention to the plank in your own eye? How can you say to your brother, 'Let me take the speck out of your eye,' when all the time there is a plank in your own eye? You hypocrite, first take the plank out of your own eye, and then you will see clearly to remove the speck from your brother's eye."
Matthew 7:3-5

These are very potent words coming from our Lord Jesus Christ. Over the years, as Pentecostals or Evangelicals we have claimed the high moral ground in as far as Christian doctrine is concerned. Any serious Pentecostal/Evangelical will tell you even in his sleep what the Catholics, Adventists, Lutherans, Mormons, Jehovah's Witnesses, Methodists, etc. are doing wrong. It appears everyone got it wrong on Christian doctrine except us the Pentecostals/Evangelicals.

We have become so preoccupied with what others are doing wrong to such an extent that no one has ever taken notice of what is going on in our own backyard!. If we are sincere in upholding the instructions of our Lord Jesus, we should also pay close attention to the above given text. Before we start looking into what others are teaching or where others are getting it wrong. It's imperative that we first pay attention to what we teach or where we are getting it wrong before we can go on to correct or teach others. According to our Lord Jesus, only hypocrites will behave as such!

There are a lot of inconsistencies between the Gospel that Paul taught the Gentile Churches and what is being taught to Gentile Christians today. Already mentioned is the fact that whatever a Church denomination or Pastors teach today must be in total agreement with teachings from the Apostles. For any doctrine to be sound, it must be compatible with the instructions that were given by the Apostles to the Gentile Churches. The Apostles gave instructions on everything that an uncircumcised Gentile Christian needs to know to live and worship in a manner that pleases the Lord.

Thus, whatever doctrine that we may teach concerning salvation, practical holiness, baptism, speaking in tongues, giving etc. must be derived from the express teachings of the Apostles.

*"Watch **YOUR** life and **doctrine** closely. Persevere in them, because if you do, **you will save both yourself and your hearers**." 1 Timothy 4:16*

*"You, however, must teach what is **appropriate** to **sound** doctrine.*
Titus 2:1
*"But as for you, teach the things which are **in agreement** with sound doctrine. Titus 2:1 AMP*
*"But as for you, proclaim the things which are **fitting for** sound doctrine."*
Titus 2:1 NASB

Paul was very particular about matters of sound doctrine. The Epistles to Timothy and Titus are regarded as Pastoral letters. This was Paul giving instructions to Timothy and Titus on how they were to Pastor their respective churches. As such these Epistles are the blueprint for all Pastors serving God under the New Testament. To Timothy, Paul instructed that he should watch closely his own life and doctrine and to persevere in them, because with the right doctrine he could save himself and the people he ministered to. One doesn't need to wonder what would happen if he neglected watching over his life and doctrine!

Timothy was not only admonished to watch the doctrine of others, but he was also instructed to be very watchful of his own doctrine. Then to Titus, Paul gave the command to teach only things that are in agreement with sound doctrine. Clearly, issues or matters of doctrine are very critical, no Pastor, preacher, teacher, or prophet under the New Testament Church has the authority to teach whatever they want. In accordance with the instructions given to Pastors, all Pastors must watch closely **their** lives and doctrine and that they are obligated to teach *only* what **agrees** with sound doctrine.

What is *"sound doctrine"* one may ask? This does not appear to be a straightforward answer since each, and every church denomination has put in place its own standards of what constitutes sound doctrine. However, the reality is that the answer is indeed straight forward. Sound doctrine is any teaching that is in total agreement with the teachings and instructions of Jesus Christ to the Gentile Churches through his Apostles. This implies that all Christian Church doctrines or teachings must be derived from the express teachings of

Jesus Christ that were given to the church through the Apostles.

Remember the circumstances that brought about the Council of Jerusalem and what the Apostles instructed all the Gentile Churches to do regarding the teachings that came from the men who had come from Judea?

*"We have heard that **some went out from us without our authorization** and **disturbed** you, **troubling your minds by what they say.**"* Act 15:24

As mentioned before, these men claimed that the Gentile Christians needed to observe the Law of Moses, starting with circumcision as well as observing Jewish customs. The whole Apostolic Council then informed all the Gentile Christians that they had heard about the men who were causing great disturbance and troubling them by what they were teaching. The Apostles indicated that these men did not have any authorization to be teaching whatever they were teaching the uncircumcised Gentile Christians. The same truth applies to all those doing the very same thing today!

The official position is that the Apostles instructed us, through the revelation of our Lord Jesus Christ and the Holy Spirit, that no one is authorized to teach the Law of Moses or Jewish Customs to the uncircumcised Gentile Christians. It then follows that anyone who pick and choose things from the Law of Moses and teaches them to Gentile Christians, would not be teaching sound doctrine!

The following verses then reveal what Paul regarded as sound doctrine or false doctrine in as far as Gentile Christian worship is concerned and what Pastors should do regarding all the people who teach false doctrine. Did the Apostle give the instruction that all those who do not teach sound doctrine or taught false doctrine should be left alone because God is the one who can judge true from false doctrine? The answer is an emphatic NO!

> *"If anyone teaches **false doctrines** and does not agree to the **sound instruction of our Lord Jesus Christ** and **to godly teaching**, he is conceited and understands nothing." 1Timothy 6v3-4*

Paul intimated that whoever does not agree with the sound instruction of our Lord to the Gentile Christian Church, teaches false doctrines. By *"sound instruction of our Lord Jesus"* Paul was referring to the instructions they had given in line with the revelation that they had received from our Lord Jesus, specifically to the Gentile Church. *"For you know the instructions we gave you by the **authority** of our Lord Jesus Christ"* (1Thess. 4:2) This is the sound instruction that Paul was talking about. Paul mentions that all those who insist on teaching false doctrines that are contrary to the sound instruction of our Lord Jesus to the Church are conceited and understand nothing!

This infers that these people lack understanding in as far as the instructions of Jesus to the Gentile Church are concerned or how the New Covenant operates in the life of a Gentile believer. These people will argue and teach truths and revelations of the Old covenant and not of the New. Paul instructed Pastors to silence or stop all the people who were teaching false doctrines about the Law of Moses to the Gentile Churches. He did not leave room for such people to be accommodated or to be left alone. Timothy and Titus were given the instruction to command such people to stop teaching the Law of Moses or Jewish myths to the Gentile Churches!

*"As I urged you when I went into Macedonia, stay there in Ephesus **so that you may command certain people not to teach false doctrines any longer** or to devote themselves to myths and endless genealogies. Such things promote controversial speculations rather than advancing God's work— which is by faith... **They want to be teachers of the law,** but they do not know what they are talking about or what they so confidently affirm."*
1 Timothy 1:3-7

*"He must hold firmly to the trustworthy message as it has been taught, so that he can encourage others by **sound doctrine and refute those who oppose it**. For there are many rebellious people, full of meaningless talk and deception, **especially those of the circumcision group. They must be silenced, because they are disrupting whole households by teaching things they ought not to teach**—and that for the sake of dishonest gain... Therefore, **rebuke them sharply**, so that they will be sound in the faith and will **pay no attention to Jewish myths** or **to the merely human commands** of those who reject the truth." Titus 1:9-14*

As one can see, Paul did not have any kind words for people who went around teaching Gentile Christians to observe the Law of Moses or Jewish customs. These people did not possess the revelatory knowledge of how uncircumcised Gentiles can properly worship God through Christ. They tried to apply their knowledge of the Law in the Jewish context to the uncircumcised believers. This was a false doctrine, and such people were to be commanded to stop doing so. Paul instructed Titus to silence and rebuke such people, for they were teaching things that should not be taught to uncircumcised Gentile Christians.

The epistle to Titus reveals various groups that were teaching false doctrines but the most dangerous appeared to be the circumcision group. As mentioned before, these were most likely Jewish-Proselytes turned Christian. Paul instructed Titus that these people should stop paying attention to Jewish myths or commands from the Law so that they will be *sound* in the faith! It then goes without saying that no minister of the Gospel was ever authorized to pay attention to Jewish myths, Jewish customs or commands from the Law of Moses as well as teaching such things to the Gentile Church.

As ministers we were given the authority through the direct instructions from our Lord Jesus through his Apostles to silence and command all those who do so to stop! Anyone who teaches Gentile Christians that they need to observe elements from the Law of Moses or Jewish customs to please God should be silenced. These people will be teaching things they ought NOT to teach. Such things or elements from the Law of Moses or Jewish customs or Jewish myths include but not limited to Sabbath observance, the ten commandments, dietary Laws, exclusive usage of the name Jehovah, circumcision, tithing, Jewish festivals, genealogies etc.

No one has the authority to teach the practice or observance of such things under the church of Christ. It is what the Apostles instructed to the Gentile Church that now regulates our worship under the New Covenant. The instructions from the Apostles to the Gentile Church are the foundation upon which all uncircumcised Christian doctrines must be established. We don't build doctrines starting from the Law to the Apostolic Instructions. We stand guided by what the Apostles instructed the uncircumcised Christians. This distinction must never be forgotten.

*Study and do your best to present yourself to God approved, a workman who has no reason to be ashamed, **accurately handling and skillfully teaching the word of truth**. 2 Timothy 2:15*

*All Scripture is God-breathed and is useful for teaching, rebuking, correcting, and **training in righteousness, so that the man of God may be thoroughly equipped for every good work**. 2 Timothy 3:16-17*

I know without doubt that most ministers use what Paul said on 2Timothy 3:16 to justify usage of elements of the Law under the Gentile Church because the bible *'says'*... *"All scripture is God breathed and is useful for teaching..."* According to their understanding, this text gave them the authority to teach any doctrine that one may think of, for as long as they have a scripture or verse for it! But is this what Paul implied, when he gave this instruction? In Chapter Two, Paul had encouraged Timothy to diligently study the scriptures so that he may accurately divide or handle the word of truth.

Secondly this verse must be taken in whole and not in part. *"All scripture is God breathed and is useful for doctrine...for rebuking, for correcting and in **training for righteousness"*** Which righteousness did Paul refer to here? Was it a righteousness that comes through the Law or apart from the Law?

*"and be found in him, **not having a righteousness of my own that comes from the law**, but that which is through faith in Christ--**the righteousness that comes from God and is by faith.**" Philippians 3:9*

Assuming we are all aware of Paul's doctrinal position regarding usage of the Law of Moses on uncircumcised believers. One can only but wonder why Paul would then give Timothy the freedom to use all scriptures in terms of doctrine formulation as he wished. Is this what Paul intended? As mentioned above, in the first Chapter of 1 Timothy, Paul mentions that one of the reasons why he had left Timothy in charge at Ephesus, was that he should command certain people to stop teaching false doctrines and on *v7* he even pointed out that these men wanted to be teachers of the Law!

"They want to be teachers of the law, but they do not know what they are talking about or what they so confidently affirm" 1 Timothy 1:7

Since Paul had instructed Timothy to command those who were teaching the Law to stop teaching false doctrines, was he now instructing Timothy to do the same? To be a teacher of the Law? Certainly, this verse (2Timothy 3:16) must be interpreted in harmony with the other texts on doctrine formulation under the Gentile Church and never in isolation!

Chapter 8

Seventh Day Adventism in light of the True Gospel.

*".... the whole SDA theology is predicated on a strong belief in the inspiration behind what they call the **"Spirit of Prophecy."** The Church believes and teaches that the writings and teachings of Ellen G. White **were divinely inspired."***

We must all understand that every Christian Church denomination or Christian movement has a founder or the person who established the ministry. In as much as Christ is the Head of the Church, he sent his Apostles to establish the Universal Church. If we want to understand more about the Gentile Church ministry, we need to pay close attention to the teachings and practices of the Apostles among the Gentiles. The same principle applies to Church denominations, if you want to understand the veracity of the Church's doctrine, one also needs to pay close attention to the teachings and practices of the people who established the denomination or ministry.

Whatever they taught or believed in must be evaluated with the teachings of the Apostles to the Gentile Church. There is no denominational church founder who is above or equal in rank with the Apostles who were given the authority by Christ to establish the Universal Church. Whoever those men or women were is not as equally important as understanding what they believed in, what motivated their beliefs and teachings. Their beliefs and teachings must then be understood within the context of the Gospel of the uncircumcised Gentile Christians.

If their teachings or beliefs were not established upon the Gospel of the Gentile Christians or upon the express instructions of the Apostles, their beliefs or teachings must be totally disregarded and be treated with the contempt they deserve. Whatever men teaches or believes about worshipping God through our Lord Jesus Christ, must be solely derived from the express teachings of the Apostles to the Gentiles. Their teachings are the foundation upon which all beliefs and teachings about Christ and Christianity must be established. This is simply because Christianity is basically the teachings from the Apostles about Christ and how we may worship God through Christ.

Christianity among the uncircumcised believers is not Judaism, nor neither is it perfected with Judaism. As is obvious to see, Judaism has always been a snare to Gentile Christians from the very beginning. Seventh Day Adventism is predicated on fostering the obedience to the Law of Moses or "God's Law" (for dramatic effect), more importantly the Seventh Day Sabbath or the fourth commandment. The Adventists believe that all the other Churches have been deceived by the devil because they have been disobedient to the fourth Commandment.

This then implies that the Adventist Church is the only true Church or the remnant Church because it upholds the *fourth*

Commandment and keeps *God's Laws*. That is roughly the long and short of Adventism. Accordingly, these beliefs must now be understood within the context of the True Gospel of Christ to the Gentiles. In line with the teachings of Christ to the Gentile Church, through his Apostles, is it true that uncircumcised Gentiles must obey God's Laws; the same Laws that He gave to the Israelites for them to uphold the Old Covenant? Did this belief emanate from the express teachings of Christ to the Gentile Church? Did the belief that all Churches have been deceived by the devil because they have disobeyed the fourth commandment come from one's understanding of the Gospel message of Christ to the Gentile Church?

What is the source of this belief? Or rather did this belief emanate from teachings and commandments that were given to the Jews or Circumcised Christians? All this fixation on God's Laws and Sabbath observance came from people who were persuaded that Christianity is perfected in Judaism or observing Jewish customs in worship and lifestyle. Before one gets obsessed with obeying the Law and observing the Sabbath, one must understand where this obsession came from. The whole idea of Adventism did not come from the express teachings of the Apostles to the Gentiles.

It originally came from a small group of people who felt that they can become better Christians if they observe the Sabbath or keep God's Law. Among many other things, they believed in the total annihilation of the wicked versus an ever-burning hell, the Levitical food laws, the ten

Commandments and the fourth command that is, the Seventh Day, Sabbath. This group of people started teaching others to do the same. They leaned quite heavily on the teachings from the Old Testament to foster their beliefs and were captivated by Old Testament prophecy especially the one in Daniel. Their leader at the very beginning was William Miller and his followers were known as the Millerites.

It is quite remarkable that all this started with just a small group of people who felt that observing some sections of the law of Moses and certain Jewish customs in particular the Sabbath, was the most Christian thing to do! They felt that Christians must observe the Sabbath and keep some parts of the Law of Moses that included the dietary laws. In essence they became Apostles unto themselves and determined how they wanted to worship and please God through Jesus Christ! Then they started teaching and encouraging others to do the same! All this did not come from their understanding of Christianity through the instructions of the Apostles to the uncircumcised Christians but their understanding of the Law.

They then tried to assimilate Christianity into their understanding of the Law. It was the Galatian Church situation all over again. Whatever this small group felt and believed in must be framed within the context of the teachings of the Apostles to the Gentile Church. It is plain to see that this group did not fully appreciate the Gospel message to the Gentiles. If they did, they wouldn't have come to all these conclusions about Gentile Christianity.

As if that weren't enough, history has it that their leader William Miller, using the Prophecy in Daniel, predicted that Jesus would come by the end of 1843. He apparently managed to convince a lot of people in New England, but this did not turn out to be true. He then changed the date to October 22, 1844. Before setting this date, Miller had set an earlier prediction that Jesus would come in the Spring of 1844 again, nothing of that sort happened.

He then predicted the date when Jesus would come to be 22 October 1844, this date coincided with the Day of Atonement on the Jewish calendar. Notably, Miller chose this date because of its connection to the cleansing of the sanctuary *in keeping with* **Leviticus 16**. The inevitable happened, Jesus did not come and the whole movement fell apart. Most of the followers went back to their original churches, including William Miller. This is known as **The Great Disappointment** in Adventism.

Miller had many zealous followers notably Ellen G. White and Hiram Edison. The Seventh Day Adventist as we know it today was then initiated by an idea that came to the Latter, Hiram Edison. It was through his teachings and of the former that the doctrine of *Investigative Judgement* was born. The other doctrines such as of soul sleep, placing emphasis on keeping the Ten Commandments, were all developed in keeping with the investigative Judgment theory. To explain away the *Great Disappointment* of 1844, Hiram and Ellen asserted that Jesus had indeed appeared on October 22, 1844.

However, he ***appeared for the first time In the Sanctuary in Heaven***. They *asserted* that *Jesus started for the first time his Day of atonement ministry in Heaven*. This was the Day that Jesus entered or went into the *Most Holy Place for the first time*. Therefore, this implied that this was the day that judgment began and not any time prior to that. The whole fabric of Adventism is woven around this bizarre teaching called '*The Investigative Judgment*'. Ellen and Edison started teaching people that Jesus entered for the first time in the Most Holy Place in Heaven on October 22 in 1844 and thus began his ***Day of Atonement ministry***!

Again, these claims that Jesus entered the Heavenly sanctuary or the most Holy place in Heaven for the first time on October 22, 1844 and began his Day of Atonement ministry in Heaven; must all be reconciled with the Apostolic teachings or instructions to the Church. To begin with, the mere fact that William Miller's protracted date of the Second coming of Jesus Christ coincided with the Day of Atonement on the Jewish calendar, leaves a lot to be desired. Secondly, on the issue of Jesus entering Heaven for the first time and beginning his Day of Atonement Ministry in heaven. Here is what the Bible says in Hebrews chapters 9 and 10.

"*When Christ **came** as high priest of the good things that are already here, he **went** through the greater and more perfect tabernacle that is not man-made, that is to say, not a part of this creation. He did not enter by means of the blood of goats and calves; **but he <u>entered</u> the Most Holy Place once for all** by his own blood, having obtained eternal redemption." Hebrews 9:11-12*

"For Christ did not enter a man-made sanctuary that was only a copy of the true one; **he entered heaven itself,** *now to appear for us in God's presence. Nor* **did he enter heaven to offer himself again and again,** *the way the high priest enters the Most Holy Place* **every year** *with blood that is not his own." Hebrews 9:24*

These Chapters reveal that Jesus' sacrifice or Atonement was a once and for all time offering as opposed to the yearly sacrifices of the Levitical priest on the Day of Atonement. They also revealed that the New Covenant had now taken effect because Jesus had already appeared in the Most Holy place in the Heavenly sanctuary and offered his blood for the forgiveness of sins. Although the authorship and date of the Epistle to the Hebrews is uncertain, it is certain that the Letter was written during the 1st century and most probably before the destruction of the temple of Jerusalem in 70AD.

It is interesting to note that, the writer described all these events in the past tense. He did not in any way imply that Jesus shall enter the Heavenly sanctuary at a later future date! He was informing his audience that all this had already taken place. Now that Jesus had finished his *one-time atonement offering* in the Heavenly sanctuary, he is now seated at the right hand of God! This was not a future event, as such it is biblically incorrect to teach that Jesus entered the Heavenly Sanctuary for the first time on October 22, 1844. Jesus does not have a *Day of Atonement Ministry in Heaven*!

The Levitical Priesthood was the one that had an annual Day of Atonement ministry and not the risen Christ! Jesus entered the Heavenly sanctuary once and for all-time when he mediated for the New Covenant over 2000 years ago!

*"But when this priest **had offered for all time one sacrifice for sins**, he sat down at the right hand of God." Hebrews 10:12*

All this is a clear indication that their teachings were only a cover up and fostered around their understanding or misunderstanding of the Old Covenant regulations for worship. This doctrine only came about, in vain attempts to explain away the false prophecies that were given by William Miller! Jesus did not appear in the Heavenly Sanctuary for the first time on October 22, 1844 and neither does he have an annual Day of Atonement ministry in Heaven!

Furthermore, what enchanted me the most about Seventh Day Adventism, is that the whole SDA theology is predicated on a strong belief in the inspiration behind what they call the *'Spirit of Prophecy'*. The Church believes and teaches that the writings and teachings of Ellen G. White are *divinely inspired*. This means that they believe that ALL her teachings and writings came from God and have the same authoritative force as the scriptures or teachings from the Bible! These writings or teachings are what they call the *'Spirit of Prophecy'*. For all the Adventists, the only way they can avoid being *'deceived'* is by paying close attention to all that was written in the *'Spirit of Prophecy'* or Ellen G. White's writings.

Losing faith in the divine *inspiration* and authority of her writings would result in apostasy. The result would be rejecting the *Sabbath (not Christ)*, turning away from God

86

and the inevitable, being lost! An obvious form of indoctrination. At the core of Seventh Day Adventism, is the subtle indication that the 'Bible' cannot be trusted. Yes, Adventists will claim to the outside world that they believe in the inspiration of the Bible, which is true, but they also believe that the bible has been corrupted by the Catholics! That is why the belief in the *inspiration* of Ellen White's writings is fundamental to their denomination. Her writings are very crucial to the SDA Church. One needs the '*Spirit of Prophecy*' to help them fully understand the Bible.

One may *not fully trust the Bible*, but one must fully and wholeheartedly trust in the inspiration of Ellen G's writings. With the subtle undertone, only believe what the Bible says after you hear what '*The Spirit of Prophecy*' says on the given text or scripture. This means that the whole Church, understands the Bible, the way Ellen G. White interpreted scriptures. *It is her interpretation of the scriptures that they claim to be inspired* and the primary basis upon which their belief is rooted. Believe everything that Ellen G. White said about the Bible because it came directly from God.

Since we are all Gentiles, this means that all of us, including Ellen G White are bound to the Gospel of Christ to the Gentiles. Despite the claims of divine inspiration to her writings, those writings and teachings must still be scrutinized and be evaluated in line with the Gospel of the Gentiles. Our Lord Jesus Christ appointed Paul as the Apostle to the Gentiles and gave him the full revelation of Gentile worship under the New Covenant. Thus, whatever Ellen believed or taught in her writings must be congruent with the revelation that was given to Apostle Paul and the other Apostles concerning Gentile worship. Paul's rhetoric to the Galatians rings a bell.

*"But even if **we** or an **angel from heaven** should preach a gospel other than the one we preached to you, let him be eternally condemned! As we have already said, so now I say again: **If anybody is preaching to you a gospel other than what you accepted**, let him be eternally condemned!"*
Galatians 1:8-9

Christianity among the Gentiles is not a matter of whimsical convictions, opinions, or beliefs. It is predicated upon the express teachings of our Lord Jesus Christ to the Gentile Church through his Apostles, that's the epitome of all Gentile Christianity. As such the Apostle Paul even went as far as instructing the Galatians not to accept him or his teachings if he started teaching things that were contrary to what he had taught them, when they first converted. He even instructed them to disregard angels from heaven that revealed another teaching that is contrary to what they had taught; Or any man who tries to teach them a different teaching about Christ, Christian piety or lifestyle that was contrary to what they had accepted from the start.

Even if someone comes claiming divine inspiration behind their teaching, if that divine inspiration is contrary to what the Apostles instructed to the Gentile Church, he or she must be disregarded. Paul understood the Law more than Prophet Ellen or her surrogates will ever do now or in the next million years to come. Paul had people arrested and killed on account of the Law of Moses and Jewish customs. That is basically the reason why our Lord Jesus chose Paul to be the Apostle to the Gentiles. Jesus knew that people like Ellen G. White would come and try to mislead many from the true Gospel. He sent someone who was more qualified and well advanced in the Law of Moses. There is absolutely no way possible that Prophet Ellen G. White understood how to incorporate God's Law under Gentile worship better than Apostle Paul and the other Apostles ever did!

Moreover, SDA eschatology teaches that all those who worship God on Sunday have the mark of the beast! They reckon that the mark of the beast is not a number but a Law. The Devil through the Pope who is the beast, has placed his mark/law on all those who go to Church on Sunday. The Roman Catholic Church through the authority of the Pope, changed God's Laws by introducing Sunday worship and changed the Sabbath from Saturday to Sunday. The Adventists have been led to believe that when Christ appears, he shall come to save the Sabbath-keepers from the beast and his worshippers. The true Church of Christ obeys God's Law, especially the fourth commandment!

Again, all these claims or teachings must be investigated in line with teachings of the Apostles to the Gentile Church. It was God through the redemptive work of Jesus Christ on the cross, who abolished the Law with its commandments and regulations for us Gentile Christians. It is God who brought about this change and absolved us from the Law not the Pope or the Catholic Church.

We make no apologies to anyone who is ignorant of this Gentile Christian worship reality. Sabbath keeping and Sabbath observance is not at all part and parcel of the Gospel of Christ to the Gentiles. This means that those who believe that they should observe the Sabbath either on Sunday or on Saturday are equally delusional. Even though Sabbath observance was very significant In Jewish worship, there is no argument about that. It would be very catastrophic for anyone to believe that the Sabbath Is equally as significant to Gentile Christians under the New Covenant.

We must understand that just because some people felt that Gentile Christians must observe the Sabbath or keep God's Laws, does not make this a biblical certainty. Gentile Christian worship is not perfected nor sanctified through practicing Judaism. People should never deceive themselves into believing that they are being good Christians through observing Jewish Customs or keeping God's Law. Just because some claim to teach from the Bible does not necessarily mean that whatever they are teaching is true, least of all inspired. God's Laws that they are so bent on keeping were the means by which Jews upheld the Old Covenant!

The prevailing opinion among the Adventists is that those who teach against obeying the Law of Moses do not fully understand Paul's message, basing on what Peter said! They assert that people misinterpret Paul's teaching because it was difficult to understand. On the contrary, Paul's message was difficult to understand to a person who was already acquainted with the Law of Moses especially among the Jews and Jewish proselytes. This is what Peter said:

> "Bear in mind that our Lord's patience means salvation, just as our dear brother Paul also wrote you with **the wisdom that God gave him**. He writes the same way in all his letters, speaking in them of these matters. His letters contain some things **that are hard to understand, which ignorant and unstable people distort**, as they do the other Scriptures, to their own destruction." 2Peter 3:15-16

First, Peter acknowledged that Paul's wisdom came from God. Paul's message was difficult or hard to understand from a Jewish perspective. His theology in general was a bitter pill to swallow for his fellow Jews. Here's why; *"When the seven days were nearly over, some Jews from the province of Asia saw Paul at the temple. They stirred up the whole crowd and seized him, shouting, "Men of Israel, help us! **This is the man who teaches all men everywhere against our people and our law and this place**."* Acts 21:27

The Jews who lived in Gentile territory were the ones who misunderstood Paul's teachings. They were circulating lies that Paul was teaching everyone against the Law of Moses or Jewish customs. The mere fact that Paul was teaching Gentiles not to observe Jewish traditions or customs of worship and lifestyle was very difficult to accept or even tolerate, from a Jewish perspective. These are the people whom Peter referred to as ignorant because they were in fact ignorant of the gospel to the Gentiles, therefore they ended up distorting Paul's teachings.

---

*Greg Taylor: Discovering the New Covenant; Why I am no longer an Adventist.

Chapter 9

Jehovah Witnessism in light of the True Gospel.

"I too was convinced that I ought to do all that was possible to oppose the name of Jesus of Nazareth." Acts 26:9

"You are my witnesses," declares Jehovah, "and my servant whom I have chosen, so that you may know and believe me and understand that I am he. Before me no god was formed, nor will there be one after me." Isaiah 43:10

For us to have a better understanding of Jehovah's Witnesses, we need not look further than what they teach and practice as a collective body in line with the teachings of the Apostles to the Gentile Church. Fortunately, their teachings are widely circulated and are in the public domain. We need to understand that their teachings come from the Watch Tower Bible Society, this is the primary source of all their teachings. The Watch Tower Bible Society was founded by Charles Taze Russell around 1871, whom upon acquaintance with some Adventist followers of William Miller, notably Jonas Wendell; had his own understanding of what Christianity should be.

He wrote small articles about his beliefs and started spreading his teachings and now over Two Million people across the globe have believed in this message. Under Charles T. Russell the Watch Tower Bible Society was merely a publishing house, and Russell's followers were known as The International Bible Students Association. The organization later morphed into something else under Joseph

Franklin Rutherford, who succeeded Russell after his untimely death in 1916. Rutherford changed the organizational structure and many doctrines of the Watch Tower Bible Society. It was no longer a publishing house only, but now functioned as the controlling body of The International Bible Society.

Because of the many proliferation of groups carrying the name Bible Society, mainly from people who were deserting the Rutherford camp. He later changed the name to Jehovah's Witnesses around 1931, the name was derived from Isaiah 43:10(captioned above) to distinguish his group from the other defectors who were using "Bible Society". He is famously quoted as saying *"It would be a name that could not be used by any other and such as none other will want to use."*

As mentioned in the previous chapter, if one wishes to ascertain the veracity of a Church denomination's doctrine, one needs to first understand the teachings and practices of its founders. What motivated their beliefs and teachings? We all must understand that these individuals were just ordinary human beings like us, who happened to have certain beliefs regarding Christianity. They then came up with their own teachings or doctrines that best reflect or augment their beliefs about Christ and Christianity and started to teach others these same beliefs.

Whatever beliefs they had about God, Jesus or Christianity must be assessed in line with the Gospel message to the

Gentiles. The epitome of Gentile Christian worship is what the Apostles instructed to the Gentile Church and not these beliefs. The mere fact that the Israelites used no other name but the name of Jehovah in their worship of YAHWEH under Old Testament Israel, is not a justification for this practice under the New Testament Gentile Church of Christ. Simply because we are now under a different Covenant.

Let me point out that Jehovah's Witnesses obsessive compulsive usage of the name of Jehovah in worship, taking pride in being identified with the name Jehovah, and even going around witnessing in the name of Jehovah, is what piqued my interest. From where I am standing, it appears to be more than obvious that the Apostles and New Testament believers witnessed in the name of Jesus and called upon the name of the Lord Jesus for salvation and forgiveness of sins.

So, where did this teaching that New Testament Gentile Christians must use and identify with the name of Jehovah in worship come from? This is what needs to be scrutinized in line with the teachings from the Apostles. Let me just explain to the best of my knowledge the Ideology behind using and identifying with the name of Jehovah and why this is very important to Jehovah's Witnesses.

They believe that Eternal life is acquired through studying the Bible and in particular through knowing God's real name, using it in worship and being identified with it. This knowledge of God's real name is what brings or gives a person eternal life. That's why knowing God's real name is at the core of their pedagogy. For them, this is a salvation issue, this knowledge is what brings eternal life. If one does not know God's real name, he or she cannot be saved!

while Jehovah's Witnesses accede that *we must believe in Jesus, they assert that our salvation is closely linked with a proper appreciation of God's real name.* To them belief in Jesus does not save anyone, it is knowledge and full appreciation of **God's real name** that brings salvation. It is they that accurately call unto the name of Jehovah, that shall be saved. Below is an extract on their theological perspective on this doctrine using what the Apostle Paul said on Romans 10:13.

"for example consider the words of Paul to the Romans, as they appear in the Authorized Version: "For whatsoever shall call upon the name of the Lord shall be saved" (Romans10v13). Whose name do we have to call to be saved? Since Jesus is often Spoken of as "LORD" and one scripture even says: "Believe on the LORD Jesus Christ and thou shalt be saved". Should we conclude that Paul was here speaking about Jesus? -Acts 16:31, Authorized Version.
*No, we should not. A marginal reference from Romans 10:13 in the Authorized Version points us to Joel 2:32 in the Hebrew Scriptures. If you check that reference, you will find that Paul was actually quoting the words of Joel in his letter to the Romans and what Joel said in the original Hebrew was "Everyone who calls on the name of Jehovah will get away safe" (New World Translation) Yes, Paul meant here that we should call on the name of Jehovah. **Hence while we have to believe in Jesus, our salvation is closely linked with a proper appreciation of God's name"***

The above captioned quote does acknowledge that in Acts 16:31 Paul clearly mentioned that *"Believe in the Lord Jesus Christ and thou shall be saved"*. Paul made it very clear that it was belief in the **Lord Jesus Christ** that brings salvation to this jailer, and then to the Romans, the same person informs the whole Church of Rome, that they should call on the name of **Jehovah** and not Jesus to be saved? The author then clearly ignores what Acts 16:31 says and then sloppily concludes that salvation is closely linked with a proper appreciation of God's name and not belief in the Lord Jesus! However, Peter also used the same text from Joel at the feast of Pentecost when more than three thousand Jews were converted to Christianity. Was Peter speaking about the Lord Jesus or the name of Jehovah?

> *"**And everyone who calls on the name of the Lord will be saved.**' "Men of Israel, listen to this: **Jesus of Nazareth** was a man accredited by God to you by miracles, wonders and signs, which God did among you through him, as you yourselves know." Acts 2:21*
> *"Therefore, let all Israel be assured of this: God has made this Jesus, whom you crucified, **both Lord and Christ.**" Acts 2:36*

Is it not plain to see that when Peter used this same verse from Joel, He was talking about Jesus and not Jehovah? Because, in verse 36 he then further explained that it was God who **made Jesus both Lord and Christ**. This is why salvation is now being acquired through both believing and calling out on the name of Jesus, for God has made him both **Christ and Lord**. In fact, Peter gave numerous Old Testament *Hebrew* scriptures that spoke about the **Lord** in reference to Jesus Christ of Nazareth. He was most definitely talking about the name of Jesus and not Jehovah.

Conspicuously, the Apostles always referred to Jesus as *'The Lord'*. Whenever they used the term *'the Lord'* either in writing or in speech, it was always referring to Jesus. Thus, in line with the teachings of the Apostles, salvation comes through belief and calling on the name of the Lord Jesus Christ and not Jehovah. Knowing God's real name of Jehovah is not a salvation issue in line with the teachings of the Apostles to the church! Why did Jesus die on the cross if all that we needed was to just know God's real name to be saved?

According to the people who developed the Jehovah's Witnesses dogma, the whole of Christendom has fallen into apostasy for lack of frequent usage of the name of Jehovah in worship. For them, the indicator for the true worshippers of God, is the frequent usage of the name of Jehovah. They assert that the name of Jehovah was deliberately omitted from the Greek translations or copies of the Bible. They further assert that this occurred around the third century, that's when the apostasy crept into the Christian Church. All these assertions must be ratified by the scriptures.

However, absence of the name 'Jehovah' particularly in the New Testament Greek scriptures or even the fact that Christians do not use the name Jehovah frequently doesn't imply that the Church has fallen into apostasy. This change was brought about by God, as Peter pointed out in the above captioned texts from Acts 2:36. Christians now use and identify with name of Jesus in worship and for salvation, under God's instruction. The Jews were given the name of Jehovah in their worship under the Old Covenant. Christians on the other hand were given the name of Jesus in their worship of God under the New Covenant! All this was done by God, but under two separate Covenants. That's why Paul made this declaration in his letter to the Philippians.

"Therefore, God exalted him to the highest place and gave him the name that is above every name, that at the name of Jesus every knee should bow, in heaven and on earth and under the earth, and every tongue acknowledge that Jesus Christ is Lord, to the glory of God the Father."
Philippians 2:9-11

It must be understood that fixation on the name of Jehovah and exclusive usage of Jehovah is a well-known and well-established Jewish custom in keeping with the Law of Moses. No one disputes the fact that Jews were given the name of Jehovah in their worship of God under the Old Covenant. Hence, this doctrine came from individuals who clearly misunderstood or had very little knowledge of the dynamics of the New Covenant worship. For starters, the mere fact that Old Testament saints or even Jesus used the name of Jehovah doesn't at all imply that those who use God now instead of Jehovah are wrong.

Moreover, the New Testament is centered on the person and name of Jesus Christ, the son of God. This change was only instigated by God himself; He is the one who elevated and exulted the name of Jesus! It is quite unfortunate that those who came up with this doctrine perceived the usage of the name of Jesus and absence of the name of Jehovah as reluctance or apostasy on our part.

*"But you will receive power when the Holy Spirit comes on you, and will **be my witnesses** in Jerusalem and in all of Judea and Samaria and to the ends of the earth" Acts 1:8*

Nothing could be further from the truth, we use and associate ourselves with the name of our Lord Jesus Christ because that is what He instructed, through the express instructions he gave to the Apostles before his ascension. These are direct words from Jesus, he instructed his disciples or Apostles to go and be his witnesses around Israel and to the end of the earth. The disciples were given express instructions to go and witness in his **name** and they were going to witness about him.

Our Lord Jesus Christ did not instruct his Apostles or disciples to go and be Jehovah's Witnesses or better still witness in the name of Jehovah or about Jehovah. He sent them to witness about himself. This teaching cannot be ascertained from the instructions of Jesus to both the Jewish and Gentile Christians. In keeping with the command to witness in his name, we see Peter standing in front of many Jews at the annual Jewish feast of Pentecost, boldly witnessing in the name of Jesus!

*"Peter replied, Repent and be baptized, every one of you, **in the name of Jesus Christ** for the forgiveness of your sins. And you will receive the gift of the Holy Spirit." Acts 2:21-28*

This was Peter, witnessing about Jesus and in the name of Jesus to his fellow Jews who were used to the exclusive usage of the name of Jehovah in worship. There is also another incident that happened and was recorded in the 3rd

chapter of Acts. The incident took place at the Beautiful gate, at the temple, when Peter and John, had healed a man who had been born a cripple. Did Peter and John call on the name of Jehovah for the man to be healed? The answer is a definite No! This miracle was performed in the name of Jesus and they got into serious trouble with the Jewish Priests and religious leaders for doing so.

> "Then Peter said, "Silver or gold I do not have, **but what I have I give you. In the name of Jesus Christ of Nazareth, walk.** Taking him by the right hand, he helped him up, and instantly the man's feet and ankles became strong. He jumped to his feet and began to walk. Then he went with them into the temple courts, walking and jumping, and praising God." Acts 3:8

> "When Peter saw this, he said to them: "Men of Israel, why does this surprise you? **Why do you stare at us as if by our own power or godliness we had made this man walk?** The God of Abraham, Isaac and Jacob, the God of our fathers, **has glorified his servant Jesus...** **By faith in the name of Jesus,** this man whom you see and know was made strong. **It is Jesus' name** and the faith that comes through him that has given this complete healing to him, as you can all see." Acts 3:12-16

As is obvious to see, the Apostles were witnessing and performing miracles in the name of Jesus. They were declaring the name of Jesus every chance they got. Apparently, this did not go down well with the other Jews who believed that nobody should be teaching or declaring any other name except that of Jehovah. Peter and John were arrested by the priests and were forced to appear before the Jewish Sanhedrin that was presided by the High priest. When they appeared, this was the charge they had to answer to:

*"They had Peter and John brought before them and began to question them: "By what power **or what name** did you do this?"*
Acts 4:7*

The Jewish religious leaders wanted to establish what name they had used in healing the man who had been born a cripple. To that, Peter boldly and emphatically declared:

*"Then Peter, **filled with the Holy Spirit, said to them:** "Rulers and elders of the people! If we are being called to account today for an act of kindness shown to a cripple and are asked how he was healed, **then know this, you and all the people of Israel: It is by the name of Jesus Christ of Nazareth... Salvation** is found in no one else, **for there is no other name** under heaven given to men by which we must be saved." Acts 4: 8-12*

Please note that Peter made this bold declaration when he was full of the Holy Spirit. When the Jewish religious leaders enquired about the name they had used, he needed to think carefully before he could give an answer. If he dared speak of any other name save the name of Jehovah, death was certain. Nevertheless, even when full of the Holy Spirit, he did not say anything about the name of Jehovah, but boldly declared that they had used the name of Jesus of Nazareth! It was because of the name of Jesus the man who was born a cripple stood before them, fully healed.

Furthermore, he declared that salvation is found only in the name of Jesus. For there is no other name under Heaven **given to men**, by which we may be saved apart from the name of Jesus. *Salvation is NOW found in no other name*, except the name of Jesus! **It is God** who gave us the

101

permission to use the name of Jesus in worship and attaining salvation. The Sanhedrin couldn't do anything to Peter and John because the people were praising Jehovah for what had happened, and the man was also standing before them completely healed.

What did they do instead? They had no other option but to let them go, they also commanded them not to speak or teach in the name of Jesus and gave them stern warnings and threats. Wait a minute, so Peter and John, were commanded and threatened not to witness or use the name of Jesus in their worship by the High Priest and all the other religious leaders? Were they threatened for using the name of Jehovah? Were they commanded not to use or witness to anyone in the name of Jehovah? No! They were commanded not use the name of Jesus!

*"Then they called them in again and **commanded them not to speak or teach at all in the name of Jesus.**" After further threats they let them go. They could not decide **how to punish them**, because all the people were praising God for what had happened."*
Acts 4:18-21

However, the Apostles continued witnessing and teaching in the name of Jesus. Later, Peter and John were arrested again and appeared before the Sanhedrin for the second time. This time the crowd was a bit riled up and on the Sanhedrin's side. Therefore, the unanimous opinion was that the pair should die for continuing to witness and teach in the name of Jesus and not Jehovah, like they were commanded by the Law.

These men were witnessing in the name of Jesus and the whole of Jerusalem was giving in to their message.

"We gave you strict orders not to teach in this name," he said. "Yet you have filled Jerusalem with your teaching..." Acts 5:28

This time around, the Jewish religious leaders wanted blood! Gamaliel, a well-respected teacher of the law counselled against killing the two Apostles and the whole Sanhedrin relented. The Sanhedrin then decided to have them flogged and released instead. Consequently, the Apostles were once again reprimanded and ordered not to witness or teach in the name of Jesus, again!

"His speech persuaded them. They called the apostles in and had them flogged. **Then they ordered them not to speak in the name of Jesus** *and let them go. The apostles left the Sanhedrin, rejoicing because they had been counted worthy of* **suffering disgrace for the Name.**" Acts 5:40-41*

Is it that difficult to perceive which name the Apostles witnessed or used in their worship and identified with? In some circles the Apostles were even identified as the blasphemous Jesus of Nazareth followers or the Nazarene movement. The Apostles faced immense persecution from the very beginning of the Church for using the name of Jesus in their worship. As the above captioned texts from the first few Chapters of Acts can reveal, the Apostles were commanded not to witness or teach anyone in the name of Jesus. After appearing before the Sanhedrin, Peter and John were publicly flogged for using the name of Jesus. The pair left the Sanhedrin rejoicing because they had been counted worthy to suffer disgrace for the **name**! Which name was this? Of course, it was the name of Jesus!

> *"And he has come here with authority from the chief priests to arrest **all who call on your name**." But **the Lord said to Ananias**, "Go! This man is my chosen instrument **to carry my name** before the Gentiles and their kings and before the people of Israel. I will show him how much **he must suffer for my name**." Acts 9:14-1*

The above is an exchange between our Lord Jesus Christ and Ananias. Ananias was protesting about going to pray for Saul, because he had travelled all the way to Damascus from Jerusalem to arrest everyone who called upon the name of Jesus. Then our Lord reassured him that he shouldn't worry or fear for his life, because He had chosen Saul to be his chosen instrument to carry **His name** that is, the name of Jesus, amongst the Jews and Gentiles and that Saul shall also suffer greatly on account of that **name**! Which name was he going to suffer for and **carry** among the Gentiles? Was it going to be the name of Jehovah or the name of Jesus?

These are just a few references from the first few chapters of Acts, and I am more than certain that I have made my point! First, the Apostles were given a direct command by Jesus to go and be his witnesses or to go and witness in his name. The above captioned texts give full proof evidence of how the Apostles obeyed this command and started witnessing and teaching in the name of Jesus. I can even go so far as giving further reference throughout the New Testament writings so that we may accurately determine which name Christians must use in worship and the name that brings salvation.

I must also point out that the following scriptures are all direct quotes from our Lord Jesus. He was thus referring to his name, the name Jesus and not Jehovah!

*Matt 18v20 "where two or three are **gathered in my name**, I shall be in their midst"*

*Matt 18v5 "and whoever welcomes a little child like this **in my name** welcomes me."*

*Mark 9v39 "Don't stop him, Jesus said, for no-one **does a miracle in my name** can in the next minute say anything bad about me"*

*Mark 9v16 "I tell you the truth whoever gives you a cup of water **in my name** because you belong to Christ will certainly receive his reward."*

*Mark 16v17 "and these signs shall accompany those who believe. **In my name** they will drive out demons, they will speak in New lounges"*

*John 14v13 "And I will do whatever you ask in **my name**, so that the son may bring glory to the father. You may ask me for anything **in my name** and I shall do it"*

*John 14v26 "But the Counselor, the Holy Spirit whom the father **will send in my name**, will teach you all things and remind you of everything I have said to you."*

*John 15v16b "Then the father will give you anything you ask **in my name**"*

*Jhn15v21 "they will treat you this way **because of my name**, for they do not know the one who sent me."*

*Acts 9v15 "but the Lord said to Ananias "Go. This man is my chosen instrument **to carry my name** before the gentiles and their kings and before the people of Israel...""*

*Revelation 2v3 "You have **persevered** and have **endured hardships for my name** and have not grown weary."*

The following scriptures captioned below are quotes from the teachings and instructions from the Apostles that shows how they used the name of Jesus in worship and everyday life.

*John 20v31 "but these were written that you may believe that Jesus is the Christ, the son of God and **that by believing you may have life in his name**."*

*Act 8:12 "But when they believed Philip as he **preached** the good news of the kingdom of God and **the name of Jesus Christ**, they were baptized, both men and women."*

*Act 9:27 "But Barnabas took him and brought him to the apostles. He told them how Saul on his journey had seen the Lord and that the Lord had spoken to him, and how in Damascus **he had preached fearlessly in the name of Jesus**."*

*Act 19:17 "When this became known to the Jews and Greeks living in Ephesus, they were all seized with fear, and **the name of the Lord Jesus was held in high honor**."*

*Act 21:13 "Then Paul answered, "Why are you weeping and breaking my heart? I am ready not only **to be bound, but also to die in Jerusalem for the name of the Lord Jesus**."*

*Act 26:9 "**I too was convinced that I ought to do all that was possible to oppose the name of Jesus of Nazareth**."*

*1Co 1:2 "To the church of God in Corinth, to those sanctified in Christ Jesus and called to be holy, together with all those everywhere **who call on the name of our Lord Jesus Christ--their Lord and ours**:*

*1 Corinthians 5v4 "When you are **assembled in the name of our Lord Jesus Christ**"*

*Ephesians 5:20 "always giving thanks to God the Father for everything, **in the name of our Lord Jesus Christ**."*

*Colossians 3:17 **"And whatever you do, whether in word or deed, do it all in the name of the Lord Jesus**, giving thanks to God the Father through him."*
*2Thessalonians 1:12 "We pray this so that **the name of our Lord Jesus may be glorified in you**, and you in him, according to the grace of our God and the Lord Jesus Christ"*
*1Jo 3:23 "And this is his command: **to believe in the name of his Son, Jesus Christ**, and to love one another as he commanded us."*
*Hebrews 13v15 **"Through Jesus** therefore let us continually offer to God, a sacrifice of praise- the fruit of the lips that **confess his name."***

According to the above given verses, we learn that we have life by believing in his name. Philip and Paul preached in the name of Jesus, the name of Jesus was held in high honor among Jews and Greeks living in Ephesus. Paul was ready not only to be arrested but to die for the name of Jesus. This is the same Paul who once tried to do everything *to oppose the usage of the name of Jesus of Nazareth in worship*. Christians everywhere call on the name of the Lord Jesus Christ, believers assemble in the name of Jesus...etc.

As Paul once confessed that he once tried to do everything possible to oppose usage of the name of Jesus of Nazareth in worship, this is the same thing that Jehovah's Witnesses are now doing. This desire to oppose usage of the name of Jesus came from Paul's Jewish theological perspective of worship. Using the name of Jehovah in worship, prayer or witnessing is not a Christian thing, but a Jewish custom. This compulsive usage of the name of Jehovah is diametrically opposed to the direct teachings of our Lord Jesus Christ, that he gave to the Church through his Apostles.

As uncircumcised Christians worshipping Jehovah under the New Covenant, we use the name of our Lord Jesus Christ in everything we do. It was this usage of the name of Jesus instead of Jehovah that angered the Jews and the Jewish religious leaders and motivated them to persecute Christians. Identifying with the name of Jehovah pretty much defies and undoes everything that our Lord taught and that which all the Apostles died for. There is nothing Christian at all about using the name of Jehovah in worship or witnessing, as this teaching did not come from either our Lord Jesus Christ or his Apostles.

As mentioned at the beginning of this chapter, the name Jehovah's Witnesses was derived from Isaiah 43:10 by Rutherford. The golden rule is always that, whatever we practice today as Christians must solely be predicated upon the express teachings of Jesus Christ to the Gentile Church through his Apostles. It is quite unfortunate that Jehovah's Witnesses take pride in being disgraced for using the name of Jehovah, even though this practice of using and witnessing in the name of Jehovah isn't a Christian thing. Knowing and using the name of Jehovah in worship isn't a salvation issue.

The mere fact that some people assert it to be so, doesn't make it true. The instruction to Identify and Witness in the name of Jehovah came from Rutherford and not from Jesus or the New Testament teachings to the Gentile Church! Hence, one can only but wonder, how knowing God's name became a salvation issue. Instead of embracing and identifying with Christ or the name of Jesus, people are being taught to shun it and identify with the name of Jehovah, instead. The command to worship and use the name of Jehovah in worship was given to the Jews under the Old Covenant and not to uncircumcised Christians.

As Christians, we were given the name of Jesus Christ and were instructed to use the name of our Lord Jesus in our daily life and in worship, under the New Covenant! This teaching of doing everything, witnessing, and even attaining salvation in the name of Jehovah, is at odds with the Gospel message.

Source "Wikipedia; Jehovah's Witnesses"
Lesson 1 What is the Good News
Lesson 2 Who is God?
Why we should know God's name?
God's name and the "New Testament"
God's name and Bible Translators
Christians and the Name
The Divine name through the Ages
"Hallowed be Thy name"-What Name?
God's name – it's meaning and pronunciation

In conclusion...

If a doctrine cannot be founded purely on what the Apostles instructed the Gentiles, it is a false teaching. It doesn't matter who is teaching it, for how long they have done so, or how many people they have managed to convince! It does not matter which denomination you belong to; this principle is universal. We only have one Jesus and one true gospel. You must do whatever you can to make sure that you believe in the right Jesus and the true Gospel that came directly from Jesus through his chosen Apostles. This is what the Apostle Paul said at one point...

> *"For if someone comes to you and preaches **a Jesus other than the Jesus we preached**, or if you receive a different spirit from the Spirit you received, or **a different gospel from the one you accepted**, you put up with it easily enough. And I will keep on doing what I am doing in order to cut the ground from under **those who want an opportunity to be considered equal with us** in the things they boast about. For such people **are false apostles, deceitful workers, masquerading as apostles of Christ.**"*
> *2 Corinthians 11:4, 12-13*

"...those who want opportunity to be considered equal with us.." These people had become Apostles unto themselves, coming up with their own beliefs about Christ and Christianity as they considered themselves to be equal in rank with the Apostles. They then went about teaching these beliefs to the believers. Paul described such people as deceitful workers who masquerade as apostles of Christ! We have had so many such persons among us for so long, that most of us have been led astray by beliefs and teachings of such people. We stand guided and instructed by the written Apostolic instructions to the Gentile Church of Christ!

www.ingramcontent.com/pod-product-compliance
Lightning Source LLC
Chambersburg PA
CBHW062003040426
42447CB00010B/1892